50

On Puget Sound and Pacific Coast

A Memoir
By Captain Gerald Bell

Copyright © 2015 by Gerald R. Bell

Worked for four different companies on waters between Los Angeles and Ketchikan from 1959-2010

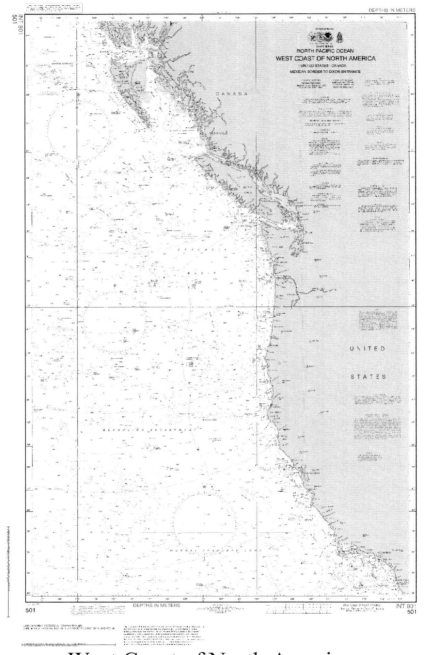

West Coast of North America
(Alaska - Southern California)

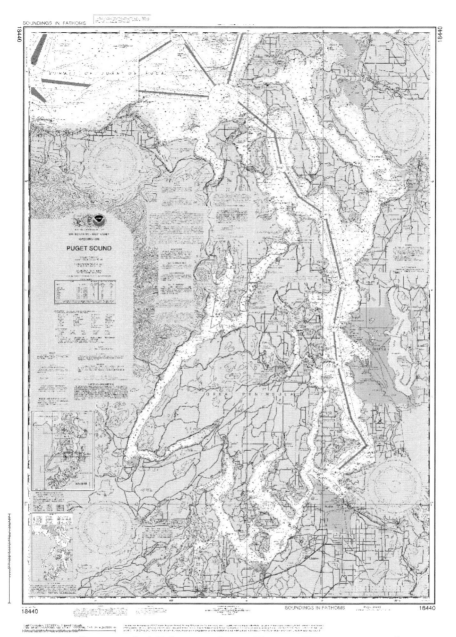

Puget Sound (Olympia - Port Townsend)

Acknowledgment

I would like to thank the many people who have helped me on this voyage through book writing. First, Jana Gage who nudged me into starting this project. Claire Swedberg and the participants in her Creative Nonfiction writing class at the La Conner senior center carried me through to the end with friendly and enthusiastic editing and encouragement.

I had help with editing from several people. Patrick and Esther McLatchy, Pat did the first complete edit and made numerous suggestions on how to improve my writing. Big thanks to my family for their support with a little extra thanks to Knut my son for his expertise. Claire Swedberg did an edit for me. Then Janna Gage did two more final edits. There were others who helped me along the way that I have not mentioned, but I'm sure you know who you are. I thank you all from the bottom of my heart.

Disclaimer
The stories in this book are from my memory and they may not be the same as you remember them.

CONTENTS

Dunlap Towing tug just through
Deception Pass with log tow
(Photo by Murphy Hektner)

PART – I (1959 to 1969)
The Early Years

1. Go to work at Dunlap Towing, 14
2. *Malolo*; Trip with *Skagit Belle*, 16
3. Log Towing; Bellingham trip and cold weather, 22
4. Log Towing; beachcombing logs, 28
5. Log Towing; Port Ludlow, fell off tow, 33
6. Freight Barging, 37
7. Dunlap Towing Tugs, 47
8. Lost Freight Boat; tandem towing, Stick Point, 48
9. Move to *Vulcan* as Mate, 51
10. Ran over by barge, 53
11. Falling to sleep on watch, 55
12. Log towing; tow breakup in Canada, 58
13. Drafted into the Army, 61
14. Fishing in Alaska, 65
15. Back home and trip to Kansas, 72
16. Back to work; gravel barging, 75
17. Wind Storm, 3 man crew *Pacific Foam*, 79
18. Towing Gravel and Saturnalite, 83
19. Interesting happenings, near miss on buoy, lose tow wire, cut electricity to Guemes Island, 86
20. Captains job; barge roll over, 90
21. Move to *Kiket*, start building new barges, 95
22. Crew on *Kiket*, ship and barge collision, 99

PART – II (1970 to 1998)
Puget Sound Freight Lines

23. Start with PSFL, Info on *Narada* and *Kiket*, sinking of *La Conte*   103
24. Landing with tug alongside barge,   110
25. Tug crew, remodeling of *Kiket*, start building tugs,   113
26. Wind Storm Seattle Harbor, Port Townsend. Port Angeles, Wind at Discovery Bay,   119
27. Cooks on tugs,   124
28. Back on *Kiket*, Puget Sound freight barging, storm at Point Wilson,   128
29. Move to the *Edith Lovejoy*, freight boat captains, Powell River trips,   133
30. Predicting tide current for travel route, Swinomish Channel Bridge,   136
31. Operators license and test, traffic lanes,   141
32. Tug *Andrew Foss/Pachena*, trips to Portland, Oregon,   146
33. Predicting weather for Port Alberni trips, wind storms,   153
34. Tug *Duwamish*, barge Cape Flattery, Hawaii trips,   159
35. Tug *Duwamish*, Port Alberni and Gold River trips, fire on *Duwamish*,   162
36. After the fire,   167
37. Close calls,   170
38. First trip to California,   175
39. Second trip to California,   178
40. Start tandem towing,   182
41. Interesting things on the water,   188
42. Boat maintenance and failures,   193

Part – III (1998 to 2005)
Olympic Tug and Barge

43. The end of Puget Sound Freight Lines; start Olympic Tug and Barge, 196
44. Olympic Tug and Barge; rough trip in Rosario Straits, 201
45. Willapa Bay job starts, 206
46. Willapa Bay job problems, 210
47. *Lela Joy* sinking, 214
48. Move to Tug *Lela Joy*, 217
49. Move to Tug *Alyssa Ann,* 220
50. Relived of duty, 225
51. Tug *Lucy Franco*; fueling cruise ships, 229

Part – IV (2006 to 2010)
Pacific Northwest Marine Services

52. Resign from Olympic; start at Pacific Northwest Marine Services, 234
53. Starting work on *Anne Carlander*, 238
54. Scrap Metal and Marijuana discovery, 245
55. Barge almost sinking underway, 249
56. Water in the cargo area, 252
57. Encountering storms between Tacoma and Fraser River, 256
58. Fraser River challenges, 261
59. Three incidents that got the attention of the Coast Guard, 265
60. The last trip and retirement, 271

Tugboat Life by Gerald Bell
Introduction

The tugboat is a versatile work horse. Its varied uses include ship handling, (moving ships into and out of docks); towing logs or barges, (cargo barges, sand and gravel barges, oil barges, log and wood chip barges, construction barges) and escorting oil tankers.

The first tugs appeared in the early 1800s and were steam powered. In the 1900s steam gave way to large, slow turning, direct drive, diesel engines. These direct drive engines could be reversed by stopping the power and shifting the cam, (usually with air). There were two sets of lobes on the cam one for forward and one for reverse. The cam is a shaft in the engines that has raised areas called lobes. When the shaft turns these humps contact the valve stems causing the valves to open, to exhaust and close for the next firing of the cylinder.[1]

In the 1940s, smaller, more compact high speed diesel engines with reverse gears came into use. A more recent development is the tractor tug. Tractor tugs assert the same amount of force, forward and reverse and sideways, in all directions. The newest addition to the tractor tug model is the hybrid tug. These tugs shut down the diesel engine automatically when power demand is low and run off electric power supplied by batteries to save fuel.

---

[1] Wikipedia

Tractor tugs come in two types of propulsion; cycloidal and Kort nozzle. The cycloidal propulsion propeller consists of a series of vanes positioned in a circle pointing downward. The system adjusts the pitch of the vanes to throw the wheel wash in a given direction to coincide with the operator's demands from controls in the wheelhouse. A Kort nozzle is a propeller surrounded by a cylinder that is adjustable 360 degrees.

There have been other changes as well. In the 1950s and 60s tugboat companies transitioned from wood hulls to steel and then from single to two engines and two propellers (known as twin screw). Horsepower has been increasing from a few hundred to 3000 to 5000 and higher. Wood hulls have been phased out and single screw tugs are limited in what they can be used for because insurance will not cover them for some work.

My 50 years on tugs spanned the time of small, single screw, wooden hull tugs with manual steering, a magnetic compass and few crew conveniences, to today's modern steel hulled, twin screw tugs with all the conveniences of home. I saw our navigation tools transition from a magnetic compass, binoculars and a spot light to the marvelous electronic instruments in use by today's mariners.

The new powerful tugs today incorporate crew comfort with electronic controls and navigation. Electric/hydraulic steering systems are incorporated with auto pilots and radar, electronic charts, GPS and AIS that can all be contained in one unit. GPS is satellite navigation and AIS is Automatic Identification System. AIS use VHF radio to receive and transmit information about all vessels within VHF range, about 20 miles.

When I started work on tugs fifty years ago, successful, on-the-job experience is what moved a sailor up to captain. Licenses weren't required for the small tugs (less than 200 gross tons) which I worked on. Today's wheelhouse personnel are required to have licenses and a tugboat endorsement that sometimes takes several years to obtain, with written tests to pass, and can include four years of college. A captain of a large ocean-going ship cannot get on as a captain of a tugboat without this endorsement. Of which, on-the-job towing experience is required.

In my fifty years of sailing Pacific waters I have seen the number of boats and ships increase greatly. Just as the traffic increased on land so has the traffic on the water. When I began work there was very little traffic with slower moving vessels around Puget Sound. Today, with designated traffic lanes and fast moving ships, things can get congested at times. In areas like Partridge Point on the west side of Whidbey Island in Washington state's Puget Sound where four traffic lanes converge it can get down right challenging. I have encountered several vessels there at the same time, including huge, fast moving ocean going ships, fishing vessels, private yachts, tugs and barges and anything from submarines to aircraft carriers of the U.S. Navy. There are no stop lights on the water.

As a child, I never once dreamed of being a tugboater. After I boarded my first tug, that's all I wanted.

Tugboats are a common sight on our Northwest waters. But few non-tugboaters know much about them. I hope my story will help change that.

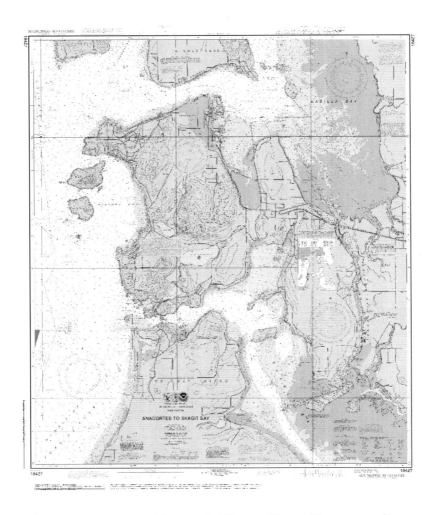

Anacortes to Skagit Bay (La Conner is on the right at the South end of Swinomish Channel

PART - I
Tugboat Life (1940 to 1959)
Chapter 1
The Early Years

I had a 50 years career working on tugboats on Puget Sound and the Pacific Coast waters. Because I grew up near the small coastal town of La Conner, in western Washington, it was fairly easy to get a job at Dunlap Towing, a local tugboat company.

I graduated from high school in the spring of 1958. I started classes at Skagit Valley College that fall and soon realized I was wasting time and money with no clear goal in mind and fairly poor grades. At the end of the first quarter I dropped out of college and got a job at a local pea processing plant sacking frozen peas. Maybe I should go into farming? I had done some farm work for my dad and uncle and some of the local farmers during and after high school.

In the fall of 1959 a good friend and I were hanging out with nothing to do like every typical Friday night. We decided to apply for a job at Dunlap Towing in La Conner. As time passed and I had not heard from them, I forgot about it. Then one day I got a call from Dunlap. They asked if I was still interested in a job on a tugboat. Of course I said "yes" and I was told to show up for work the next morning.

The next day I arrived at Dunlap's office at the appointed time. I was assigned to Captain Manfred

Nystrom. Manfred gave me a paint scraper and put me to work scraping the bottom of the tug *Ora Elwell*, which was sitting out of the water on a grid at the side of Dunlap's shop on Swinomish Channel in La Conner.

Now this paint scraping got old real quickly and I begin to wonder if this was what I had been hired for. At lunch time Manfred took me to the Waterfront Café and told me to order whatever I wanted on Dunlap's tab. After lunch we loaded up in a car and headed for Camano Island. We stopped at a beach on the west side of the island. The tug *Malolo* was passing by with a log tow. At about the same time a small rowboat departed from alongside the tug and headed our way with one man in it.

John Allen was decrewing because his wife was about to have a baby. So John came to the beach with all his gear and I loaded up my gear and rowed back out to the tug. The crew onboard consisted of Captain Richard Dalan and two other crew members. I entered this situation like a fish out of water. Like a lot of people starting a new job I had not a clue of what I was suppose to do. When I asked Richard what my tasks were he said "Enjoy the scenery and you can learn as we go."

I don't remember much about that first trip but I think we delivered that log tow to Everett. It was the beginning of a long love affair with tugboats and working on the water.

Tugboat Life (1959-1969)
Chapter 2
Malolo: Trip with *Skagit Belle*

The tug *Malolo* was a 50 foot wooden tug with a small diesel engine, single screw. Crew accommodations were sparse. It had a very small galley, wheelhouse, captain room, head (bathroom), crew's quarters, and engine room. These spaces were only accessed from out on the deck. In other words you had to go out into the weather to go from the galley to the wheelhouse or any other place on the vessel.

Tugs before the 1960s were simple compared to the modern tugs of today. The *Malolo* had a small, direct reversal, diesel engine. Direct reversal engines had no reverse gear. The engine had to be stopped and the engine cam shifted so that it would run in reverse then restart. This was accomplished with two manually operated levers in the wheelhouse; one for stopping, starting, and throttle and one to shift the cam so the engine would run in reverse. Small cables connected these levers to the engine and ran through a series of pulleys down to the engine room.

The galley had the only sink and a diesel stove. The head had a toilet, no shower, no sink. The toilet had to be flushed with a bucket. This meant going out on deck and dipping water from the side of the boat. If the boat was moving it could be like dropping a fifty pound weight at the end of the rope you had attached to the bucket. I learned to toss the bucket ahead, attached to a short line, and then yank it out of the water before the line came tight because of the forward motion of the boat.

Accommodations included a captain's room with a small, single bunk and a crew's quarters with four bunks. The crew's quarters were below and up forward in the bow. The bunks were built-in cubby holes with a curtain to draw across for privacy.

The wooden deck dried out in the summer and would shrink and open up cracks. Water on the deck from rain or waves seeped through and dripped into the crew space below. If the deck stayed wet for a period of time the wood would swell and these cracks closed back up. In the meantime we nearly needed rain gear in bed to stay dry. We filled these cracks with a cotton material called stuffing. The process included pulling out some of the old stuffing and pounding in new, then pouring hot tar on top of the stuffing. Over time, with expansion and contraction, the cracks opened and we had to do it all again.

The navigation equipment consisted only of a magnetic compass, spot light and binoculars. Most of the inland and harbor tugs had no radar or fathometer. In some areas like rivers and channels, sounding boards were still in use when I began working. A sounding board was used to determine your position in low visibility. Sounding boards (or echo boards) were placed in shallow waters where the channels were narrow. They were solid rectangular shapes placed on piling facing the boat's line of approach.

The position was determined by sounding the horn until an echo returned. Once the position was determined a course was charted to the next course change. Radars and fathometers started showing up in the mid 1960s. These were both welcome improvements that made navigating easier but the mariner had to be careful not to rely too heavily on just one of these sources of information. The rule of check and double check still applied.

Not long after going to work on tugs I was a deckhand on a trip on which we had to use an echo board. I was crewed on the tug *White Bear* with Captain Tom Rock and two other crew members. We were towing the decommissioned sternwheeler, *Skagit Belle,* from Seattle to Mount Vernon loaded with packages of tinplate for the Mount Vernon Carnation milk plant. As we approached the mouth of the Skagit River we ran into fog. Unable to find the channel entrance without radar we decided to anchor and wait for the fog to lift. We headed west towards Whidbey Island with all hands watching ahead for the beach. Suddenly one of us looked up and saw trees above us even though we couldn't see the beach ahead. We immediately stopped and dropped anchor.

After a period of time we were able to continue into the river with the help of the horn and a sounding board. The fog had lifted enough that we could see both sides of the river. Then a mile or two further up, we ran back into fog and ended up grounding the *Skagit Belle* on a sandbar. Before we could pull her off, the tide started to drop and she settled down on top of a large stump on the bottom of the river. The stump poked a hole through the hull and she filled up with water and settled to the bottom. It was quite shallow so the water didn't reach the deck. Being new to all this I don't think I fathomed the consequences of the situation for the captain and the company. It was just a big adventure for me.

I was left on guard aboard the *Skagit Belle* while the tug went to retrieve a small barge to transfer the cargo to shore. The small barge was brought alongside and the cargo was transferred to a dock a short way up the river. From there it was trucked to Mount Vernon. This took a couple of days so I went from tug boating to driving a truck for a short time.

The *Skagit Belle* was later refloated and became a floating restaurant on the Seattle waterfront during the 1962 Worlds Fair. She sank at the dock in Seattle after the fair and was eventually turned into scrap.

Skagit Belle, sunk in Seattle

Skagit Belle

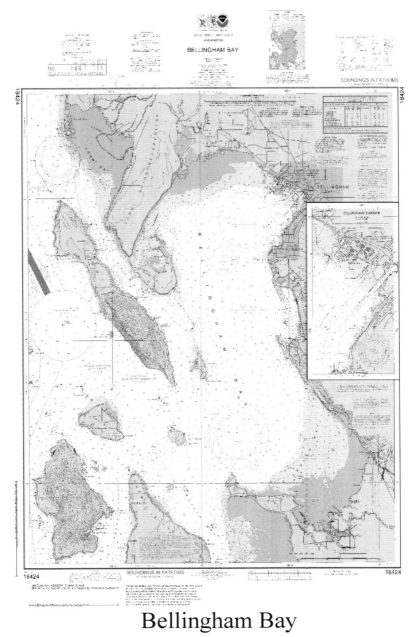

Bellingham Bay

Tugboat Life (1959-1969)
Chapter 3
Log Towing: Bellingham Trip and Cold Weather

Logs were a big part of Dunlap Towing Company. Our business included sorting, storing and building log tows for delivery to customers. Dunlap had several large storage areas around the La Conner area. Logs were delivered by truck or by water then sorted and assembled into log tows. A tow was built with a skeleton of logs called boom sticks. Boom sticks consisted of logs 60 ft. to 80 ft. long with a 4 inch diameter hole drilled in each end about 1 ft. from the end. The boom sticks were held together with "boom chains" to form a rectangle one stick wide and several long. These were called rafts and stretched anywhere from one to eight boom sticks long. Each boom stick length was a section. (For example, a tow of four boom sticks long would be a four section raft.) The sides were held parallel to each other with a cable or a boom stick running across the tow and attached to the end of each boom stick, called a swifter. A cable was a wire swifter and boom stick was water swifter. A boom stick on top of the logs was called a top rider. After the log tow reached its destination and the logs were extracted from the water the boom sticks were returned to be made into a new tow.

Log tows were pulled at about 1.5 to 2.5 knots average speed; one knot equaling 1.15 miles per hour. Log tows were vulnerable to damage from wind, waves, and tidal current. Weather forecasting was not as refined back then as it is today, so a tug captain had to use his local knowledge and experience to know when to be moving a tow or when to wait for the tide or weather. Sometimes several days could be spent waiting for weather.

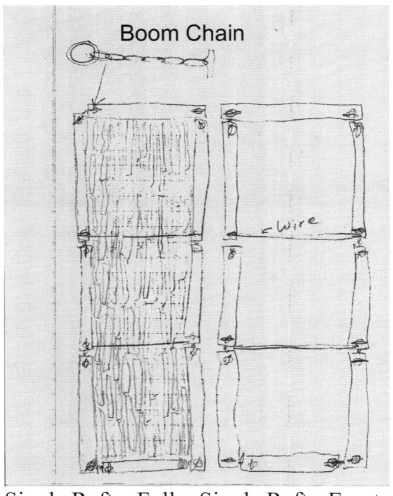

Single Raft – Full   Single Raft - Empty

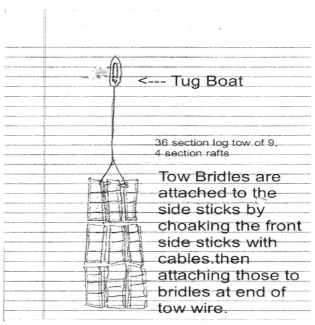

Tow with 9 Rafts

I "crewed up" in Port Angeles once during bad weather and after two weeks we had moved the log tow to Discovery Bay where we then decrewed, a move of about 25 miles. On another occasion we spent our whole two week shift tied to Dog Fish Island at the north end of the Gulf Islands in Canada. Time was spent checking the weather channels, listening to the chatter of other tugs talking about the weather and we managed to fit in some exploring and hiking the Island. Then, there is always the normal cooking and cleaning up of meals and keeping living spaces clean. We had to be prepared for these kinds of delays, with enough food, water and fuel.

This brings to mind a trip in the 1960s when we ran out of everything! I was about 20 or 21 years old and being used as captain occasionally on short trips. We left La Conner with me and a crew of three on the tug *Crosmor* for what should have been a two day log tow from Bellingham to La Conner. At Bellingham we constructed a tow of several log rafts. As we were finishing, the northeast wind started to blow and the temperature plummeted from the low fifties into the twenties.

After getting under way, I turned the helm over to the mate and laid down for a little rest. A couple of hours later I was awakened by the movement of the boat so I got up to see what was happening. The wind had increased to about 25 knots and the swell was starting to build. We decided not to keep going ahead because the swell would just get worse and there were no good places to hide ahead of us. We turned around and headed for Chuckanut Bay a distance of three or four miles.

To turn a large tow with a swell running it is necessary to either slow down and pull gently or take a wide sweeping turn at a reduced speed. I used the slow gentle turn. After a couple hours we were in a sheltered area and in shallow water where we dropped anchor.

Then we were hit with a different problem. The northeast wind was blowing maybe 30 knots through the bay and the temperature kept dropping. Because of the frigid temperature our water pipes froze and we lost all of our potable water. It also froze the diesel fuel line to the galley stove. We were not sure how cold it got because we had no thermometer on board but it hurt to breathe without face protection. By this time we had no drinking water and had run out of food. We were able to unthaw the diesel to the stove and cooked about ten crabs that we found in a crab pot caught in the tow and we had some canned fruit juice to drink. We were in radio contact with our office but the weather was so bad that they couldn't get relief to us for a couple of days. Our office kept our families informed of our situation. The roads ashore were covered with ice and snow so it was decided not to send supplies via car or truck.

A relief tug, the *Narada,* from La Conner had to plow through ice in the Swinomish Channel. Upon arrival at our position their crew went out on deck to drop the anchor. To accomplish this they had to turn a handle to loosen the "brake shoe" and let out the anchor chain. The handle was connected to the brake shoe with a one inch shaft and when they turned the handle the shaft snapped off because of the extreme cold. They had to use a pipe wrench to turn the shaft. In about thirty minutes we had the tow turned over to the other tug and we were headed home to our great relief. We tied-up at the Dunlap shop in La Conner. The shop crew told us to head home and they would take care of any repairs. We had taken this job on our time off between Christmas and New Years Eve, for which I had made reservations, but because of the weather delay we were gone through New Years. My wife was not too happy about this but she soon learned that this is what can happen when your life is subject to "changing weather conditions".

.

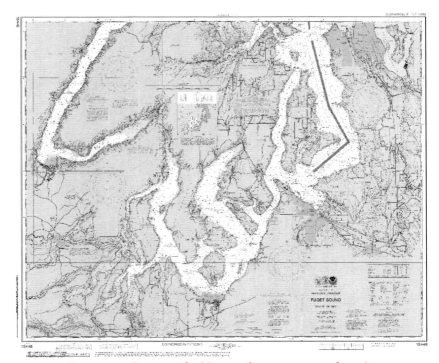
Puget Sound (Southern portion)

Tugboat Life (1959-1969)
Chapter 4
Log Towing: Beachcombing Logs

Log towing can be an interesting adventure. Crews usually begin with lots of hard work putting a tow together. Many hours or days pass to reach the destination. Then there is more hard work to tie the tow up and remove any safety gear that has been installed at the beginning of the tow.

Safety gear is important and includes chains or cables installed at weak joints between boom sticks for reinforcement, with "dog gear" stretched across the exposed ends of the tow. Dog gear consists of chains or cables strung through several dogs. A "dog" is an arrowhead shaped piece of metal with an eye on the large end. The "dogs" are driven into every log across the end section of the tow and into the side boom sticks with an axe, that has a sharp end on one side and a flat hammer head on the other side. Dog gear is used in areas of the tow that are exposed to wave action, usually at the end of the tow.

Cork boots were worn (boots with metal spikes protruding out the sole) for work on the logs. Putting dog gear on large logs is fairly easy. But a tow with small logs could be challenging. To cross a tow with small logs it was necessary to keep moving or your weight would sink the logs. Getting the dogs into the logs was like dancing a ballet. If you were too slow you got extremely wet.

We towed in and out of numerous places around Puget Sound and the San Juan Islands. Most of these places at that time were still undeveloped and pristine. Places like Port Ludlow, Port Gamble, Pleasant Harbor, Quilcene in Hood Canal and Chambers Creek in the Tacoma Narrows. In the San Juan Islands, Deer Harbor, East Sound and Humphrey Head come to mind as well.

Occasionally a log tow would break apart while under tow and a large amount of logs would drift free. If this happened at night the logs might be spread over a large area before the loss was noticed. Even if all the normal precautions of safety gear, choosing the correct tides, and avoiding bad weather were taken, losses still occurred. It was part of doing business and would not reflect on the crew's ability unless it happened often.

The towing company would have to put together a crew to go retrieve those wayward logs that were washed up on beaches in a short time. This process usually involved a shallow-draft tug to pull the logs off the beach and another tug to collect and raft up the recovered logs. Logs are branded by their owners when they are cut down in the woods. A heavy hammer with the company's brand is used to smack the end of each log to leave a permanent impression. If a log has no brand it is owned by the State. This means every log on a beach or adrift is owned by someone.

I was involved in two of those recovery operations over the years. One was along the Swinomish Channel and I was the guy on the beach to hook a line onto each log so it could be pulled into the water. The other time was on Whidbey Island just north of Oak Harbor. This time I was running the tug that was holding onto the logs that were collected. At the end of the day when we had collected all the logs we could find, my deckhand and I still had to tow the logs to Similk Bay and tie them up while the other tug and its crew headed home. The current was running against us and it was going to take us all night.

As we passed the south end of the Swinomish Channel the boom sticks around the logs broke apart and we started to lose them again. I had felt a slight surge when it broke and quickly took the boat out of gear. The deckhand went back to pull in the towline as I backed up to the tow. In the excitement of the moment I backed faster than he could pull in the line and the line washed under the stern and got wrapped in the propeller. So there we were, dead in the water, our log tow slowly falling apart. The only thing I could think to do was to tie both ends of the line down and shift the gear in forward then reverse several times to shred the line into pieces. That worked and the pieces were spit out of the prop. We were able to patch up our tow with the loss of only a couple of logs. After a long day and night we got back to the dock in La Conner and headed home.

A log tow transiting through Swinomish Channel at La Conner, Washington.

Log tow underway through Deception Pass on the North end of Whidbey Island. (Washington State)

Tugboat Life (1959-1969)
Chapter 5
Log towing: Port Ludlow, fell off Log tow

My first few months of work for Dunlap were spent towing logs. Because a tug works 24 hours a day, some time is spent working in the dark. On one night we were departing Port Ludlow with a tow of logs that had several extra boom sticks tied along-side. Because the sticks were fanned out from the tow we decided they needed to be tied in against the side. The captain let me off with a pike pole, a flashlight and some tie line and continued towing out of the harbor. I managed to get the center portion of the boom sticks secured and was working on the tail end. The captain had the spotlight on to illuminate the logs, then he suddenly turned it off. This left me in the dark with no night vision on a moving tow.

I started to lose my balance and made a leap for the boom stick that I had been trying to secure. I missed and went into the icy cold water. I didn't have on a life vest and had on heavy cork boots so I don't know how hard it would have been to swim a long distance but I managed to grab the last boom stick at the end of the tow as it was going by. If I had missed I would have been left floating alone in the dark and with only the captain in the wheelhouse driving the boat. Who knows how long it would have been until I was missed. Regardless, I did manage to get back on the logs and finish securing the sticks to the tow.

I'm not sure if this dunking was lack of experience or bad luck. I remember a story told to me by Ron Peterson about his experience of falling off a log tow. It happened during daylight hours at the port dock in Anacortes. Ron, the deckhand, and Bill Ishmael the captain on the tug *Jerry D,* were delivering a tow for export. As they were preparing to tie the logs to the east end of the dock Ron left the tug and ran across the logs to tie them to a dolphin. When he reached the far side he failed to stop and ran right into the water. He went straight to the bottom, sank into the mud and was stuck there. He was a few feet below the surface and couldn't get free. On the tug Bill had not seen him go overboard and wondered what happened to him. Bill quickly tied the tug to the tow and ran across to find Ron and saw him underwater. He was able to reach down and pull him free. Even with scary happenings like this everybody managed to survive.

Tools of the trade

Pike Pole - used to push or pull

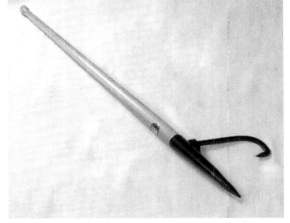

Peavey - used as pry bar and for rolling logs

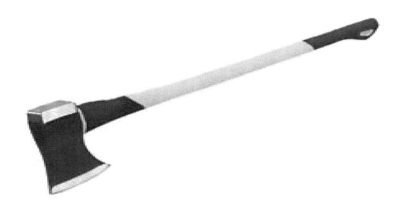

Single bladed axe

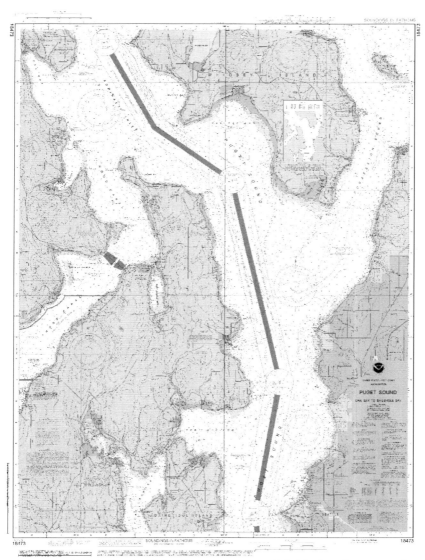

Chart #18473 (Oak Bay to Shilshole Bay)
Port Ludlow is to the upper left

Tugboat life (1959-1969)
Chapter 6
Freight Barging

In the early 1960s Dunlap Towing and Puget Sound Freight Lines formed a company called Merchants Transportation. Dunlap supplied the tugs and crews and Puget Sound Freight Lines provided the barges. In the beginning they used some of their old small freight boats as barges. These small freighters harkened back to the end of an era that started with the Mosquito Fleet in the 1850s. The Mosquito Fleet consisted of numerous small steam powered vessels that hauled freight and passengers all over Puget Sound from Bellingham to Olympia during the 1850s to the 1930s.

The first white settlers had arrived in Puget Sound in the 1840s. The first American steamboat called *Fairy*[2] arrived onboard the sailing vessel *Sarah Warren* in 1853[3] and was lowered into Puget Sound on October 31. She made her first published trip on November 12. She made runs twice a week between Olympia and Steilacoom and once a week between Olympia and Seattle. The fare was $5 to Steilacoom and $10 to Seattle, a high price for that time period.

After the 1930s diesel powered freighters took over. Puget Sound Freight Lines started in 1918 with the 65

---

[2] Wikipedia
[3] Wikipedia

foot *Chaco* and came to have several of these small freight boats serving large and small communities around Puget Sound. Most of these vessels had one cargo hatch with a cargo elevator. They had eight to fifteen crew members per vessel. Compare this to a tug crew of five and you can see the reason for converting these manned vessels to unmanned barges. A program of building new steel barges with aluminum houses began and the old freight boats were phased out as the barges came on line.

Colman Dock - Seattle 1912[4]

Yesler Wharf - Seattle 1882[5]

[4] Wikipedia
[5] Wikipedia

The interstate highway system had not been built yet and the freight that would later be hauled by truck was being moved by water. This freight included items that might be purchased at a Sears store, as well as canned fish, canned vegetables, appliances, beds and mattresses, beer and hard liquor, some pulp and paper products and more.

Until the 1930s, the cargo was loaded and unloaded with the use of hand trucks. Puget Sound Freight Lines pioneered the use of gas-powered forklifts with all of the freight on pallet boards in the warehouse ready for loading. The tug crews did all the loading and unloading of the barges using forklifts. They were paid a cargo handling wage for this work along with their tugboat wage.

The freight boats had elevators run by compressed air. The crew picked up loaded pallets with forklifts then drove out of the warehouse and onto the elevator via a ramp. The elevator operator lowered the elevator to the main cargo deck and the forklift driver drove onto the cargo deck and stowed the pallet. The cargo had to be stowed in correct order to accommodate loading and unloading at stops along the route of travel. These freight boats had a lower covered deck and an open upper deck. The crew covered the cargo stowed on the exposed upper deck under tarps if rainy weather was expected during transit. I was working on the tug *Crosmor* when we started towing those freighters. We made runs up and down Sound stopping at many docks along the way. A typical run included loading freight at Pier 62 in Seattle; general freight, empty tin cans and cases of beer. Then we headed up to La

Conner to unload the empty cans at the fish cannery, located south of the Rainbow Bridge, and loaded pallets of canned packed salmon. Next we moved to Puget Sound Freight Lines dock, north of the bridge and loaded canned vegetables. After departing La Conner it was a short hop to the Anacortes City Dock where we unloaded inbound freight and loaded canned salmon and other outbound freight. The next stop might be Bellingham to discharge beer and other freight. After loading any outbound cargo, we then headed back to Seattle via either the Swinomish Channel or outside Whidbey Island and in through Admiralty Inlet.

All of these short hops between docks meant very little rest for the crew, so the longer runs were a good time for the crew to catch up on rest. The mate and the two deckhands did most of the cargo work. The captain and the cook helped some of the time but made sure they got enough rest to drive the tug. Each tug had two crews and the work was divided into two weeks on and two weeks off. After two weeks of long hours and occasionally bad weather we were all ready for some time off. These were desirable jobs in the company because a crew member could make twenty to thirty percent higher wages, than just tug pay, since cargo work was paid extra above the tugboat wages. The cargo hours we worked were pooled together and split evenly among the crew.

Working on a tug, towing freight barges, could mean long hours of work and very little sleep. Cargo work sometimes took the whole crew working 18 hours straight or more. After getting underway, the "wheel-

Belana

Skookum Chief

(Early freight ships of Puget Sound Freight Lines)

Indian

F E Lovejoy

(Early freight ships of Puget Sound Freight Lines)

watches" were divided up among the whole crew - sometimes, with just one man on watch.

One dark night, the mate woke me to take over the wheel watch. I arrived in the wheelhouse still somewhat asleep. The mate pointed out our position on the chart and navigation light ahead and to our left which he said was Marrowstone Point and said I should keep off to my left. After the mate left I noticed the lights of a large ship far off to my left. This is where I thought Marrowstone Island should be so this started to worry me. As I approached the light I turned on the spot light and, WHOAAA! Nothing but land ahead of me and to my right, I suddenly realized from the chart that this was Bush Point and I needed to keep it to my right. A few more minutes and I would have been aground on a very unfriendly rock strewn beach.

With a little more experience and training I would have noticed this mistake earlier. All navigation lights have their own characteristics by the color of the light and the duration of time between flashes. These characteristics are noted on navigation charts. The lesson learned was to never trust anything, even though the information was from an experienced mate, check and then double check. None of the tugs had radar at this time so we relied on familiar land masses in daylight and on clear nights. During cloudy dark and moonless nights we used a compass and navigation aids, including lights, horns and bells on points of land and buoys.

There is an old tow boater saying that goes something like this – "Tow boating consists of long monotonous hours occasionally interrupted by seconds of PURE PANIC!"

My first job on one of these freight runs was at a warehouse in Tacoma. Being unfamiliar with the equipment, forklifts and flatbeds, I started out by practicing driving around the warehouse without any cargo. Since it was a Sunday, the warehouse was empty except for the tug crew. I began by trying out a flatbed; a lifting machine with a bed in front, about 7 ft. long and 4 ft. wide, and a platform in back with a raised control station which contained the steering wheel and other hand controls, between the driver and the lifting platform. The operator stood on the control platform. When hauling cargo we usually traveled backwards, because the cargo blocked your vision forward, so the steering was normal in that direction. Turn right and you went right and turn left and you went left. But going forward you turned left to go right and right to go left.

I started practicing driving slowly, picking up a few things and setting them down. As I got a little braver I started driving faster. I was driving forward down a long straight aisle when I suddenly lost control. When I tried to turn right by turning the wheel right, the machine turned left and headed for a 15 foot stack of cargo. In a split-second decision all I could think to do was jump off. The machine had a pad on the floor that the driver stood on and when the weight left that pad the brake was activated so the machine came to a quick stop about 3 feet from the pile of cargo. If I had hit that cargo it probably would have fallen on top of me with very bad results. Feeling quite humiliated I looked around to see if anyone had seen this stupid mistake. No one had, so I got back on and was soon confident enough to start helping with the cargo loading. The fork lifts were much easer to drive; they were more like driving a car.

This method of the tug crew handling cargo came out of an agreement with the Longshoremen's Union many years before and was called the 'Wetback Agreement'. The term "Wetback" in this case was a nickname for a ship's crew members. It allowed the crew to handle cargo in just one of the hatches on multiple hatch ships for extra pay. The shipping companies started building one hatch ships so the crew could handle all the cargo themselves. This agreement only allowed these ships to stop at private docks and not at port docks. The agreement changed in the early 1980s during a recession to give the longshoremen more work. We were allowed to stop at port docks and unload and load our cargo but when unloading we were allowed only to move the cargo into the warehouse and set it down. Then the longshoreman did any high piling that was needed. I never did get too comfortable with hauling cargo before a change came along - of which, I'll explain later.

Vulcan

Malolo (left) and the *Crosmor (right)*

Tugboat Life (1959 to 1969)
Chapter 7
Dunlap Towing Tugs

The tug being used in the late 1950s was the *Crosmor*, a single screw with a small Caterpillar diesel engine. Some of the other tugs that Dunlap owned were the long haul tugs *Vulcan*, *Pacific Foam*, *Narada*, *Malolo* and harbor tugs *Ora Elwell* (named after Forest Elwell's daughter), *Martha*, *Gerry D* (Gene Dunlap's daughter), *Nick* (Dunlap's dog), *Ethel* (Gene's good friend's daughter, Ethel Miller) and *Suzie*. The *Vulcan*, *Pacific Foam* and *Malolo* were being used for log towing and gravel barging and the *Narada* and *Crosmor* for freight barging.

Ora Elwell

Tugboat Life (1959 to 1969)
Chapter 8
Lost Freight Boat: Tandem Towing Stick Point

The beginning of the freight boat business was a learning time for all involved. The process of handling the cargo, picking up loads and moving cargo without damage was one part. The second part, towing freight barges, was evolving as time went by.

On one trip from Seattle to La Conner we were asked to tow two of the old freight boats at the same time. The first one was hooked to the tow line from the *Crosmor* and the second barge to the back of the first with a single heavy line. This worked fine until the southeast wind started to blow when we were nearly to La Conner. The line connecting the two together began to take heavy strain from the wind and swell. As we rounded Strawberry Point, better known as 'Stick Point' locally, on Whidbey Island, at about 0300 the line parted and the rear barge took of by itself downwind and into shallow water where we could not retrieve it.

The wind had picked up to 50 or 60 knots. The captain called the night dispatcher in La Conner for help. The loose barge was being pushed along by the wind at a good clip northward across shallow water at the mouth of the Skagit River. Directly in the path of that loose barge was a rock jetty at the south end of the Swinomish Channel, next was a large fish trap in

Martha's Bay, consisting of two lines of piling with netting that led the salmon into an enclosed area where the fish were collected.

Because of the very high tide the barge managed to pass over the top of the jetty and headed for the fish trap. The Dunlap dispatcher had kicked two crew members out of bed in La Conner. They raced down to the dock and got under way on the tug, *Jerry D*. After exiting the Hole-in-the-Wall they turned right into Martha's Bay and managed to corral the loose barge when it was just a few feet from the fish trap. It had traveled 7 or 8 miles in about an hour and a half. If it had not been stopped it would have plowed through the trap like a knife through warm butter. The damage would have depended on what part of the trap was hit.

In the meantime, on the *Crosmor,* the wind was still blowing like the "mill tails of hell" as we continued down towards the south end of the Swinomish Channel with our remaining barge. When we tried to turn right into the mouth of the channel the wind blew us across and onto a sandbar. The barge drew more water than the tug so it ran aground before the tug ran out of water. We then had to wait for the next high water to continue on to La Conner.

The assist tug delivered the runaway barge into La Conner and tied it up. The wind had dropped by the time we were able to pull the grounded barge off the sandbar and continue on our way to LaConner.

It would be quite awhile before we tried tandem towing again. For me as a new deckhand it was a big adventure and I had no thoughts of the consequences involved with the near disaster.

Tugboat Life (1959 to 1969)
Chapter 9
Move to *Vulcan* as Mate

I was 20 years old (in my second year at Dunlap Towing) and was just getting used to the freight handling business, when a big change came along. The company changed from a non-union to a union company and I was asked by Don Sanford, dispatcher, if I would like to be a mate. Still being new to the marine business my thought was -- what does a mate do? Until then there had been a captain and a crew. I accepted the position of mate on the tug *Vulcan* with Captain Tom Halle.

The crew on the *Vulcan* consisted of two deckhands, a mate and the captain. The mate's job was to be in command when the captain was off shift. The captain had the 0600 to noon and the 1800 to midnight watches, while the mate took the noon to 1800 and the midnight to 0600 watches. A license was not required for the captain or the mate for tugs of less than 200 gross tons. (This requirement was still ten years down the road.) Most deck officers obtaining a license now are attending four years of college or going to a private "sea school" in their local area. These sea schools take from four to six weeks, followed by two to four years of on-the-job training. It has been estimated that it costs around $25,000.00 (or more) to obtain a license through a sea school and of course much more for four years of college.

The *Vulcan* was mainly engaged in log towing in and out of Canada and around Puget Sound. Towing several hundred logs around and through the San Juan Islands and Gulf Islands with all of their rocks and tidal currents takes lots of local knowledge that is often learned through hard knocks, both comical and frightening. A lot of the tows destined for Canada were pre-staged at Deer Harbor on the west side of Orcas Island by other tugs in the company. The tows out of Canada southbound sometimes stopped there or continued south to other destinations.

Tugboat Life (1959 to 1969)
Chapter 10
Run over by barge

A brush with death occurred about this same time on a day job at the south end of the Swinomish Channel. I was working on a small pile driving barge with Roger Nelson and Chuck Hedlund. The barge had a tower at one end and a winch with a cable leading up the tower to raise and drop a large weight, called a hammer which drove the piling into the ground. We were using the tug *Nick* to move the barge around to replace piling for the log storage east of Goat Island.

The process was for the tug to shift the barge into position then the tug would select the correct size log from a log tow. The log was hoisted up the tower via the cable and secured into place against the tower then driven into the mud with the hammer.

On completion of our day's work we were moving the barge into a mooring position to tie it up for the night. As we approached the "tie-up", I was on the barge and crossing the front end heading to grab the line. Most of the barge had wooden planks on the deck and because we had been working with logs I had cork boots on with steel spikes on the sole. At the front end of the barge was an area of bare steel and when I stepped on it my feet slipped out from under me. I fell hard, half on and half off the barge, and then rolled off into the water. The barge was moving forward and ran over me!

I can remember seeing lots of bubbles rising up then I came up against the bottom of the barge. I pushed myself away and started swimming not knowing which way to go. It was dark under the barge but soon it got light and I broke the surface alongside the barge. Chuck was standing on a "bumper log" tied alongside and grabbed me. He literally jerked me straight up out of the water! I think the adrenalin was flowing in all of us. Other than feeling very foolish, my only damage was scratches to my hands from barnacles on the bottom of the barge. And of course, I got soaking wet. If I had been knocked unconscious I don't even like to think of the consequences.

Tugboat Life (1959 to 1969)
Chapter 11
Falling Asleep on Watch

An incident that I was not involved in (but that sure left an impression on me) occurred when a crew was towing a freight barge from Seattle to La Conner. Due to long hours of work, and lack of sleep, a crew member fell asleep while at the wheel. People don't think that this is dangerous on the water but it just as dangerous as a truck driver falling asleep while driving down the freeway. This incident occurred north of Everett. The tug and the barge ran aground east of the south end of Camano Island. This happened at night and at nearly high tide so they were unable to free themselves and had to wait 10 to 12 hours to get underway. The sleeping crew member suffered some damage to his pride but the tug and the barge suffered no permanent damage - only time lost.

I can remember some dark nights in the wheel house by myself when lack of sleep or boredom tried to get the best of me. I usually stood up and walked around or stuck my head out a window into the cold night air. One night I had started to feel drowsy so I was standing up and leaning against the steering wheel looking out the back window when my eyes closed, my head drooped, and I fell momentarily asleep. When I awoke with a jerk I thought, I'm going to run into that object I see ahead of me. I started flailing around with my hands to find the steering wheel. Of course the steering wheel was behind me and what I was seeing was the barge I was towing.

I had the same thing happen to me on another night. I was leaning against the steering wheel looking out the side window when I momentarily dozed off. I awoke thinking I was going to run into a point of land I was just passing.

Later during the years 1970 to 1998 working as captain I spent a large percentage of my time on shift alone on local runs to Port Townsend, Port Angeles and Tacoma. During the early 1970's we had five-man crews, the fifth man being the cook. The cook prepared three meals a day and did cargo work as well as standing watch with me part of the time. When we went to four-man crews and the cook was eliminated the deckhand then became deckhand/cook. From that time on I spent the first six to eight hours of a trip on shift by myself. So the remainder of the crew, who had done all the cargo loading and unloading, could catch up on their rest. Most of the local runs were less than eight hours.

During the time on watch by myself I did the navigating, kept the log book, monitored the radios and checked the spaces below. To make these checks I made sure my course ahead was clear of traffic and restriction and then took a quick walk through the engine room. The local runs were usually timed for an 0800 arrival at a mill or dock so most of these trips were at night.

When we got newer boats, there were alarm systems to monitor tank and bilge levels, engine functions and fire alarms. We had other larger tugs that made longer duration trips and had fulltime engineers who stood watch with the captain and monitored the rest of the vessel below the wheelhouse.

Strait of Georgia and Strait of Juan de Fuca, Gulf Islands and San Juan Islands

Tugboat Life (1959 to 1969)
Chapter 12
Log Towing: Tow breakup in Canada

Log towing is a complex specialty in tug boating that I found to be very interesting. The mate was in command of the vessel when the captain was off watch. Watches were six hours on and six hours off. The mate usually had the noon to 1800 and midnight to 0600 watches. As a mate it was my job to check the tow for any weak spots that might cause a tow to break apart underway. It was also my job to count the logs in our tow when we headed out and count it again when we arrived at our destination. Log tows come in two types around Puget Sound: "flat rafts" and "bundle rafts". Flat rafts are made up of individual logs rafted together. Bundle rafts were made up of bundles of logs. A bundle is a full truck load of logs tied together with cables. When counting a bundle tow only the bundles were counted and not the individual logs in the bundles.

We got into a routine in 1961 and 1962, towing logs into Canada then in 1962 and 1963 towing them out of Canada. I'm not completely sure but I swear some of those logs we towed north looked like the same ones that came south the next year. A lot of the departures for Canada were from Deer Harbor on Orcas Island. We pulled out of Deer Harbor and went north along Orcas Island to a point of land east of Jones Island where we waited for the tide to change. I spent so much time there on my shift that Captain Tom Halle, wrote my name on the chart on that unnamed point. He used my nickname, 'Jake', for Jake Point.

Most of our northbound tows were headed for the north arm of the Fraser River. Our route was from Deer Harbor north across Boundary Pass into the Gulf Islands. Then up to Gabriola Pass at the north end of the Gulf Islands, through Gabriola Pass and across the Strait of Georgia to the north arm of the Fraser River. Crossing the Strait of Georgia took ten to twelve hours, so we needed to look very closely at the weather. We had several places through the Canadian Gulf Islands where could hide from bad weather but to cross the open waters to the Fraser River we were exposed the whole way. When crossing the open water and the weather started to change for the worse we called for help from assist tugs. There were a few times when we had three or four Canadian tugs arrive to give us a boost into safe waters.

On one of our trips across the open water of the Strait of Georgia the weather started to turn bad on us so we turned around and headed back for the protection of the Gulf Islands. Before we could get there, the wind came up strong. This always seems to happen in the middle of a dark night! It started to blow thirty to forty knots - and it got rough.

We started to lose logs out of the tow and the bilge needed pumping but the bilge suction was plugged with something. Another crew member and I went into the engine room to try to unplug the inlet suction.

It was hot and smelly and the boat was jumping around from the rough sea. I became quite nauseated but we managed to get the pump working. We lost about three hundred logs during the storm which was nearly half of our tow! The next morning we pulled into safe mooring at the north end of the Gulf Islands. Under Canadian rules we were not able to retrieve our own logs. We had to wait for the local log patrol boats to retrieve our lost logs and we spent the next five days rebuilding our tow before we could get underway again.

Rebuilding a tow is quite a job. We were ready for work at 0800 and went out onto the tow. When the log patrol boats arrived with our escaped logs we opened the boom sticks and with the use of pike poles started rebuilding the tow to its original form. A pike pole is a long pole, 8 to 12 feet long or longer, with a metal point and hook at the end. The point is used to push the logs and the hook for pulling. After 5 long, hot days we had recovered our lost logs and were able to get underway.

Tugboat Life (1959 to 1969)
Chapter 13
Drafted into the Army

Things were going along pretty well. I was doing well for a farm kid with a high school education. I was living at home and spending my money on cars and entertainment. Then one day in May, 1963, along came a letter from Uncle Sam. I was drafted into the Army. I went to Fort Ord, California for basic training and then on to Fort Gordon, Georgia for advanced training.

Basic training at Fort Ord was okay, some of it interesting - some of it not. The rifle range was the best part for me. I had grown up shooting guns most of my life. I managed to come in fourth in our company in our final shooting test. I was awarded a cigarette lighter with a company logo on it. I didn't smoke but it was a nice keepsake.

At the end of basic training we were assigned our MOS, the military jobs, we were to be trained for. Mine turned out to be Military Police. We were loaded onto a military transport plane in California and flown to Augusta, Georgia. This was the same day that President John Kennedy was killed in Dallas Texas. We didn't hear this news until we reached Georgia in the evening. We landed at a military base and the only people around were military personnel. The main topic of discussion was that this could mean war.

During my two month at Fort Gordon I had a two week leave, so I flew home. That time at home was great. I had purchased a 1963 Corvette Stingray a few months before I was drafted and I had a girlfriend waiting for me. The time at home went by quick.

Training at Fort Gordon was mostly classroom with some field training of company sized formations for riot control. It was a time of racial unrest and there was a threat of rioters entering the base.
After Military Police training was complete I was shipped off to Schofield barracks on the Island of Oahu in Hawaii. The first six months were great. We worked only about fifty percent of the time. As a garrison company it was our job to police the base. This included gate guards and various types of patrol, foot patrol and motor patrol.

A buddy and I bought a 1953 Ford so we could explore the Island. It's a beautiful place but we were kind of limited to what we could do because our pay was about 50 dollars/month. My pay increased to 75 dollars/month before my tour of duty was up. About a month before my discharge a sergeant asked me if I would like to take the test to upgrade to a corporal. I told him no, I was going home soon and he could give it to someone else.

While we were there the Vietnam War was starting to heat up and after about six months our company was transferred into the 25th Infantry Division. Our easy garrison job turned into six days a week of Infantry/Military Police training. We got all packed up and ready to depart for Vietnam twice during the next twelve months but both times it was called off.

I discovered that if a person obtained seasonal employment you could get out of the army up to three months early. So Jerry Kausa, a friend of mine, got me a job on a fishing boat that fished in southeast Alaska and I applied for an early out. The job was available exactly to the day three months before my discharge date in June 1965. When I received my orders for transport back to California it was on a ship. This would get me back about a week late for my job. So I had to scramble around and get it changed to an airplane flight back to Oakland, California. By midday I was discharged and had caught a flight from Oakland to Seattle where my mom and dad picked me up at the airport. I managed to get back home for one night then it was off to Alaska on a fishing boat.

On my right arm is a PFC stripe and above it a 'Pineapple Lightning' patch for the 25th Infantry Division. On my right jacket pocket a sharpshooter medal.

Tugboat Life (1959 to 1969)
Chapter 14
Fishing in Alaska

I was off on a new adventure to Southeast Alaska on the fishing vessel *Duke* with Captain Jerry Hamburg and four other shipmates. The *Duke* was a 50 foot southeast Alaska purse seiner. We departed Anacortes and traveled three days via the Inland Passage to Ketchikan. Here we spent a few days preparing for the opening of the fishing season. Then it was up to Icy Straits in the northern part of Southeast Alaska for the opening day.

At Icy Straits the weather was cool and cloudy and there were seals, whales and icebergs - yes icebergs! This was the first time I had seen an iceberg. We nudged up close to a couple of them so I could take some pictures. The older hands said, "Don't worry we will see lots of icebergs this summer." Well, wouldn't you know that was the last time we saw any icebergs.

A purse seiner has a long net of several hundred feet and a powered skiff. The net is made of webbing with a "cork line" on the top to float the web and a "lead line" running along the bottom to hold the web straight down in the water. The "skiff" is towed at the stern of the fishing vessel with a line attached to the end of the net. When it is time to deploy the net the skiff is turned loose while still attached to the net.

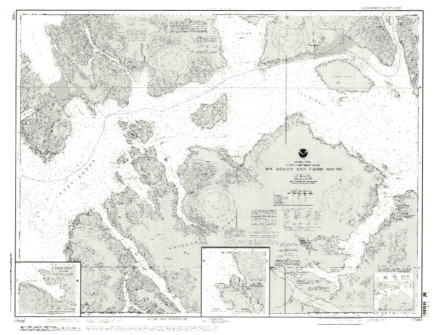

Icy Strait

Icy Strait (Southeast Alaska - June 1965)

The fishing vessel steams away causing the net to be pulled overboard. The net is held in a C shape position, thirty to forty-five minutes, or until the captain thinks it has collected enough fish and before the fish get wise to their fate and begin to escape. The two vessels tow the two ends of the net together and the skiff-man hands his end off to the fishing vessel. The skiff then positions itself on the opposite side of the fishing vessel and attaches a line to prevent the fishing vessel from becoming entangled in the net.

Fishing vessel *Duke* bringing in net

 A purse seine has a long line running through a series of brass rings at the bottom of the net. When the two ends are aboard the crew starts to haul in this purse line and the bottom of the net is closed off like a purse. After the net is closed the net is brought back aboard the vessel to enclose the fish in a small area. If the catch is too big to bring aboard all at once a large powered dip net called a "brailer" is used to dip the fish out of the net and onto the deck. The fish are stored in a compartment below in the middle of the back deck. If that area is filled the fish are stored on the deck between the back of the house and the stern. We made ten to twelve of these sets per day. The days are pretty long that time of the year in Alaska - it gets dark at about eleven at night and is starting to get daylight around three in the morning. It makes for a long day.

At the end of the day the work is still not done. We have to deliver our haul to the cannery or tender vessel. "Tenders" are stationed in areas of fishing activity and collect fish for the cannery. After unloading and cleaning the boat we tied up to a nearby dock, if available, or dropped the anchor in a quiet cove for the night. The days were long and that means the night were very short sometimes we got only two or there hours of sleep. The cook usually got to bed early so he could get up in the morning and run the boat to the next fishing ground while the rest of the crew caught a few more winks. Most of the crew caught a little rest while the net was in the water, except for the skiff man which became my job after a short period of orientation.

The skiff was a 15 foot open aluminum boat with a diesel engine and steering station in the middle. It was my job as the skiff driver to handle one end of the net. This included pulling the net off the fishing vessel and then holding it in position for catching fish. After closing up and handing off the net I kept the main boat from tangling in the net by attaching a line to it on the opposite side from the net.

Seine skiff on the stern of the *Duke*

We also carried a smaller chunk of net in the skiff called "a lead". It was not as deep as the large net and was used on shallow beaches to steer the fish into the main net. When it became time to close up the main net we cut the lead net loose and let it drift, then came back and picked it up after closing the main net. One day while bringing the lead into the skiff I was bent over and bringing it in as fast as I could through a small power block we had on the skiff. All of the sudden in came a large dog salmon tangled in the net and it lit almost in my lap. At that time of the year the dog salmon are ugly looking. They have a long snout and large teeth and are turning black and blue. I just about jumped overboard it scared me so bad. That got a good laugh from the crew.

Working in the skiff put me out in the weather, but 1965 turned out to be one of the warmest on record in Alaska and I ended up with a better suntan than I had after 18 months in Hawaii. The other advantage was I didn't have to deal with bringing in the net. The deck crew had to pile the net on deck as it came in through a power block up in the mast. They would sometimes be showered with water and stinging jellyfish depending on the wind or swell.

At the beginning of the season we were fishing three days a week so we could catch up on our rest on the other four days. This also gave us time for repairs and some sightseeing and exploring. Later on in the season we ended up fishing five days a week. Before it got too hectic we had a picnic and barbecued salmon with two other boats in front of a large glacier near Juneau, Alaska.

Halfway through the season one of the crew members had to quit. We still fished with the smaller crew. We just did some things differently and we had one less man to split the income with. As the season went on the fish became harder to catch and we got to the point where it didn't make sense to continue. We cleaned up, fueled up, and headed for Seattle.

I had grossed about twenty five hundred dollars. Not bad considering I would have made about two hundred and fifty during the same time in the army. Also I learned I liked tug boating better than fishing even though I enjoyed that summer's work and was thankful that Jerry let me have the job.

Fishing vessel *Duke*

Tugboat Life (1959 to 1969)
Chapter 15
Back home and trip to Kansas

Arriving back in Skagit County was fantastic. I had been gone almost two years. Because I was drafted I was guaranteed my old job back at Dunlap Towing but I wanted a little time off before going back to work. One of my army buddies, Don Sitka, was just getting out of the army and he asked me to fly back to Kansas and accompany him on a road trip out to Washington. So I hopped a plane to Kansas City and Don picked me up at the airport. I stayed with Don and his mom and dad on their family farm for several days. They showed me around their neighborhood. We went coyote hunting without any luck. I managed to get lost for a short time in that flat country with no protruding land masses to guide me.

Some of the counties allowed drinking and some did not so we had to go to a neighboring county to find a dance hall that served liquor. The area was mostly small farms with a few very small towns.

We soon loaded up Don's car with his worldly possessions and headed for Washington. We made the trip in three days with a little sightseeing along the way in Colorado and Idaho. He stayed with me for five days and I showed him around Skagit Valley and included a trip up to Vancouver, BC, for one evening. I introduced him to some of the local seafood, like surf smelt and Dungeness crab. I took him on a smelt raking expedition. Ideally to catch smelt you choose a high tide just before dark in the evening. We went to a beach just south of Coupeville on Whidbey Island. We used a smelt rake which is a tool that has a rectangular frame set at a ninety degree angle to the handle with a small mesh wire or net basket. We stood at the waters edge as the smelt came in small schools to spawn and we tried to scoop them up when they were right at our feet. These small fish are from three to seven inches long and have a coloration that blends right into the surrounding beach and water. For a first timer it can be frustrating when people right beside you are catching fish and you have yet to see a thing. Don managed to catch a few by raking when I let him know the fish were there. All-in-all this Midwesterner ended up having a great time.

To prepare the smelt for cooking we removed the head and insides then dipped them in beat up egg and flour and fried them in butter. Some of the smallest (3 to 4 inches) we left whole, frying them well-done and eating them skin, guts, bones and all. He wasn't too sure about eating the Dungeness crab - he called them "sea spiders". But the taste soon won him over.

I felt I had had a good break. It was time to get back to real life. Don headed for southern California where he planned to get a job and live and it was time for me to continue my tugboat career.

Home from fishing

Tugboat Life (1959 to 1969)
Chapter 16
Back to Work: Gravel Barging

It was the last part of October 1965 and it was nice to get back to work. I was crewed back on the tug *Vulcan* with Captain Tom Halle and crew. They started me as a deckhand to get reoriented and I moved into the mate's position after a short period of time. I was glad to be back at the job I had left when I was drafted into the Army but I felt bad that I was replacing Dave Otis an old friend of mine. He had to go back to a deckhand job and a drop in pay. My monthly pay at that time was $545 per month or about $6500 per year. My thought was if I could get to where I was making $10,000 per year I would have it made.

During the winter months of 1965 to 1966 we followed a pretty steady routine of Towing logs out of Canada. The winter weather could be challenging at times. But having said that we were averaging a couple of tows a week delivered. Log towing had been booming for about three years, Then came the spring of 1966. By May things started to slow down and I was laid off for the whole month of May.

Dunlap Towing had a policy of laying off single guys and keeping married men working. I had been assured that as soon as work picked up I would be put back to work. So I treated it like a vacation. Marlin Johnson, a close friend, and I took my 1963 Corvette Stingray and went on a road trip. We went to Reno then to Lake Tahoe. From there we went to San Francisco and then up Highway One along the coast and back home. I had been dating Christine, my future wife, for a few months and decided it was time to pop the question. She said yes and we decided on a September wedding.

My mother had contracted colon cancer the summer before and had a large part of her colon removed. In July my two sisters informed me that the doctor didn't think she had too much longer to live and if we wanted her at our wedding we might want to change the date. We set the new date for August 6, 1966. We were married on a very hot day in a small church in Burlington with a reception afterwards. My Mom and Dad were in attendance. Mom was in a pretty, new dress and a big smile on her face but looking frail. After we honeymooned in Seattle I went right back to work for two weeks. The day I got off work I went to visit my mother. She was in bed and not looking good. Dad said he was going to take her to the hospital and she died the next day.

I'm not sure my new wife understood what she was getting into by marrying a person who would be gone at sea 50% of the time and there were many discussions about changing occupations over the years, especially when we had small children, but we stayed with it and we are coming up on our 47th anniversary.

When I reported back to work on the *Vulcan*, I learned that her work assignment had changed. Log towing was still slow. Dunlap had picked up a contract to deliver barge loads of gravel to some of the local communities. This time on the tug *Vulcan* we had only one full-time crew so there was no rotating schedule. We usually departed La Conner at midnight Sunday and ran, "lite boat" (tug boater's term), up to Bellingham where we picked up our empty barge and took it to the gravel pit just west of Friday Harbor at North Bay. We had to wait for the barge to be loaded which took up to eight hours. This gave us plenty of time for other activities, like boat maintenance. We cleaned, chipped paint, and painted if the weather permitted. But it wasn't all work. There were other activities too, like hunting, fishing and hiking. Yes, fishing and hunting. It was a great time to be a tugboater and as time passed tugboats were getting bigger and added more crew comforts, like bigger galleys, showers and flush toilets. As the mate I arrived at work ahead of the rest of the crew and prepared the boat for departure.

This included starting and warming up the main engine and getting the heating system going so the boat was warm by the time the rest of the crew came onboard. For the next couple of years I was on shift with Ron Peterson for that middle of the night departure out of the Swinomish Channel. We had some interesting experiences with dark stormy nights and sometimes thick fog. Also there were those nights that were absolutely beautiful with the full moon making it almost as bright as daylight.

I remember one trip when I had been to a carnival and came aboard with a small furry toy animal I had won. I laid it on the dash at the front of the wheelhouse and forgot about it. We departed La Conner in a thick fog with both of us in the blacked out wheelhouse staring out the front window to feel our way out of the channel. Then Ron put his hand on that furry thing and thought he had touched a rat. He let out a yelp which scared the heck out of me; we both had a big laugh. These channel experiences would serve me well in years to come when I used the channel to avoid stormy weather in the Strait of Juan de Fuca.

After the barge was loaded with sand and gravel we delivered it to a destination, which could be Port Townsend, Port Angeles, Anacortes, Lopez Island, or Bellingham. At most of these places we waited for the barge to be unloaded, but sometimes we were sent off on another job for a day or two until the barge was ready. The sand and gravel was used mostly for road repair and construction. Our deliveries usually ended by Friday and we had the weekend off. This was my routine for the next two years.

Tugboat Life (1959 to 1969)
Chapter 17
Wind Storm, Three Man Crew on *Pacific Foam*

Part of boating is dealing with the weather. Forecasting was not as advanced as today and storms sometimes sneaked up on us. A few of them were memorable. One was on a trip coming out of Port Angeles eastbound toward Port Townsend. It was fairly calm until we reached Dungeness Spit. Then the wind started to increase and was soon blowing a gale of forty to fifty knots out of the southeast. At the east end of the spit we suddenly ran into ten to fifteen foot sharp, choppy swells. And of course it was pitch black out and raining sideways. I immediately slowed to minimum speed to maintain steerage and turned to face the waves head on. We had one empty gravel barge in tow which tends to help stabilize the boat somewhat but there is the worry of breaking the tow wire. The boat climbed up a wave and about a quarter of the boat came out of the water before it broke over the top and crashed into the hole in between the waves. I had the distinct feeling that if I did not keep my heading directly into the waves the boat might roll over. This lasted only about one hour until we were into calmer waters.

I was still a mate at this time but in the early 1960s the company started using me as a captain on small jobs. On one of my first jobs as captain when I was twenty and my two deckhands eighteen and nineteen, we left La Conner on the *Pacific Foam* to take a barge from Everett to Friday Harbor and we ran into trouble. After departing Everett we headed out through Admiralty Inlet and started across the Strait of Juan de Fuca for the San Juan Islands. It started to rain and blow out of the west. It was night time at this point and the wind had picked up to over forty knots. It got too rough to turn around and my two deckhands were so seasick they could not get out of bed. This boat had radar but there was so much water flying around I couldn't get it to work. I knew if I headed straight west I wouldn't hit anything. So all night long that's what I did.

In the middle of the night my electrical power went dead. I scurried down into the engine room to see what the problem was and found that a large brass connecting rod on the electrical panel had burned into two pieces. This did not affect the diesel engine or the manual steering; but there were no lights for oncoming traffic to see as I continued on; a black spot through the black night; sometimes feeling slightly seasick myself. After maybe an hour or two the lights magically came back on. I think the system automatically switched to battery power.

About four o'clock in the morning the rain had slowed and the wind and swell had abated slightly. I was able to spot the lighthouse at Cattle Point on San Juan Island. I had gone far enough to the west to be able to turn with the swell and get in through Cattle Pass at the south end of San Juan Island and into calm water. I think if I had been able to get off onto dry land that night I probably would not have wanted to ever get on another boat. But after tying up our barge and getting some sleep it didn't seem quite as bad.

On another occasion we witnessed a once-in-a-lifetime weather event. We were tied to the dock at North Bay (west of Friday Harbor) with a barge when the wind suddenly started to howl. We had to tow our barge away to keep from damaging the dock. The wind was blowing approximately 75 knots hard enough to create a fog of spray up to 8 or 10 feet above the water. We had no wind gauge. We estimated the speed by sticking a hand out the window or looking at the chop on the water. This was to be the only time in my whole career I was to see this strange phenomena. We tried to hide behind a small island in North Bay but it didn't work well so we headed to a bay just east of Friday Harbor and anchored up until the wind dropped down.

That was a bad storm. Another tug and its crew went down in it. During the height of the storm our captain, Tom Halle, talked to a friend of his on another tug that was traveling without a barge from Port Townsend to Anacortes. He had talked to him a couple of times but as they approached Rosario Straits, Tom could no longer get in touch with him even though he tried several times. Somebody reported them missing and the Coast Guard activated a search at first light. Debris that was identified as being from their tug was found on the beach at the south end of Lopez Island. The tug was later found and brought up from the bottom of Rosario Straits. The two people onboard were never found. All of the radio equipment originally sitting on a shelf in the back of the wheelhouse was found on the floor. The theory is that they may have hit a large log that stopped them and the swell rolled them over.

Tugboat Life (1959 to 1969)
Chapter 18
Towing Gravel and Saturnalite

I continued to tow mostly gravel barges throughout the late 1960s. We occasionally towed products besides sand and gravel. Saturnalite was one product we towed. It was a lightweight aggregate produced on Saturna Island in the Canadian Gulf Islands, just north of the San Juan Islands. It was produced by running a type of rock through a cooker. The cooker was a long metal tube six feet in diameter and thirty feet long set on a thirty degree angle. The rock was dumped in the top end of the tube that was turning so the rock worked its way down the tube and was heated to a high temperature. The product that came out the lower end was gravel that looked like lava rock and floated on water. It was delivered to a company in Seattle where it was used primarily for the construction of floats for marinas.

On one of these trips we arrived at Saturna Island on a clear, warm Sunday morning in the middle of summer. After securing the barge to their dock we had several hours to kill while waiting for the barge to be loaded. One of the people at the dock asked us if we would like to take a ride and see the island. So we shut down the boat and all piled into a pickup, some of us in the open air backend. This being a Sunday there was no traffic and everything was closed down. We soon arrived at the little community near the ferry dock. The driver/tour guide stopped near a house and said he would be right back. He came back out in a few minutes with a couple cases of Canadian beer. It seems this was the local liquor store and even though they were closed on Sunday our tour guide managed to pull off a purchase.

We had a great time and saw the top and all the sides of the island. By the time we arrived back at the boat it was nearly time to depart and we were all stepping pretty high. I don't think any of us remembered that the Canadian beer was more powerful than the beer we were used to. It was decided that I was in the best shape to drive upon departure. When we departed the rest of the crew went to bed and I headed for Seattle. This went okay for the first two or three hours; then my over indulgences caught up with me and I had to go outside and lean over the rail.

Of all the areas to which we hauled gravel Port Angeles was the most difficult. After departing the San Juan Islands through Cattle Pass with the loaded barge there was twenty five miles of open water to cross. When the barge was fully loaded with eight or nine hundred ton of sand and gravel the deck was only two or three feet above the water. It wouldn't take a very large wave before the load would start to wash overboard. We had one or two trips on which a quarter to half of our load had disappeared by the time we arrived at Port Angeles.

We encountered a different kind of problem on a trip to Port Townsend with a full load of gravel. By this time the tug *Vulcan* had radar onboard, but we were encouraged not to use it except in limited visibility because they were very expensive to repair. On this trip we departed the gravel pit near Friday Harbor and headed for Cattle Pass. I was on shift and as we approached Cattle Pass the fog started to settle in around us so I turned on the radar. In the middle of the pass the radar decided to quit working. Those older radars had a picture tube so it didn't die suddenly, it slowly faded away.

From the ghost picture on the tube I was able to chart my exact position and set a compass course to our destination on a chart. All night long we steamed ahead through the fog. By the time my shift was about done I was thinking we must be getting pretty well across the straits and approaching Point Wilson at Port Townsend. I had the fathometer running all night and all of a sudden it went from sixty fathoms to ten then back to sixty in a few seconds. This startled me at first, and then I realized what was happening. Ha! I checked the chart and there it was. A little ten fathom spot surrounded by sixty fathoms of water so I reset my course which was not far off from the original just as the captain came into the wheelhouse to take over. He said, "Okay where are we?" I put my finger on the chart and said, "Right here." He gave me a kind of sideways look and said, "Okay, we'll see." When we arrived at Port Townsend and I got up to help land the barge, the captain told me, "You were right. After about an hour we broke out of the fog and Point Wilson was right ahead of us."

Tugboat Life (1959 to 1969)
Chapter 19
Misadventures, Near Miss on Buoy, Loose Tow Wire, Cut Electricity to Guemes Island

It seems like there was always something unexpected happening when we worked around the waters of the Swinomish Channel and the San Juan Islands. One time I was on a one day trip on the tug *Vulcan* with Captain Dave Alvord. Our job was to move 75 sections of logs from the south end of the Swinomish Channel to a storage area at the north end of the channel. (In those days everybody called the channel the slough.) This tow was the largest on record. Seventy five sections stretch almost one mile when under tow. It took the help of four small assist tugs too maneuver through the S turns at the Hole in the Wall and the two bridges at the north end. The Hole in the Wall was a narrow passage about two hundred feet wide between rock cliffs at the south end of Swinomish Channel. Since that time it has been widened by removing a portion of land on the east side.

Several days before there was a boating accident and two well known local duck hunters had drowned when their small open outboard driven boat had run into a log storage area in the dark. One body had been found the next day but the other one was still missing. The man still missing had been one of Dunlap

Towing's top captains. After we had passed through with our log tow the body was soon found and it was as though our wheel wash had dislodged it from its resting place.

On another occasion I was coming out of Bellingham with an empty barge for Friday Harbor and needed to cross Rosario Strait just north of Sinclair Island. It was at night and the tide was ebbing, running hard to the south. Two navigation buoys to the west of Sinclair Island marked the east side of the deep water. As I approached the northern most buoys, I noticed that I was being set down on it by the tide. I corrected my course more to the west to clear the buoy before continuing south but to my surprise it looked like my barge and that buoy were destined to crash. I was like a deer caught in the headlights as I watched this disaster develop. It was a large buoy and could knock a hole in the barge. I shined the spotlight on the barge and, as I watched, the buoy slipped by the stern missing by about three feet. I had to sit down to settle my nerves but I had learned an important lesson about "set and drift". Set and drift, is a term used to describe being pushed or carried off course by wind or tide. The lesson learned: don't underestimate it!

There was another incident that was more comical than serious. We had departed the gravel pit near Friday Harbor with a loaded barge for Port Angeles and were crossing Salmon Bank just west of Cattle Point on San Juan Island. We sent a new deckhand out for some on-the-job training to let out more tow wire. On the *Vulcan* the tow wire was a seven eighths inch wire cable that is spooled on the tow winch drum. He loosened the brake on the winch and let the wire run out, then tightened it back down to stop it. In the wheelhouse we had gotten into a discussion about something and were not paying attention to what was happing on the back deck. There was a loud clunk. The deckhand came back into the wheelhouse to tell us that all of the tow wire had just gone overboard. Oops!! The wire is held on the tow winch by a small metal clamp, but what really holds it is at least one and one-half layers of wire left wrapped on the winch which should never be payed out.

How do we retrieve 1500 feet of seven eight's inch wire from the bottom? We had a couple of things going for us. One, it was daylight and calm, and two it was in fairly shallow water. We started at the barge end of the cable and fished up the end that was attached to the barge bridles. After detaching the tow wire from the barge bridles we were able to get enough slack in the wire to take some wraps around the capstan on the side of the winch. Then it was just a matter of hauling all the cable aboard and piling it on the back deck. Then we could reattach it to the tow winch and spool it back where it belonged. This whole process took three or four hours with the help of everyone onboard.

Then there was the time we killed all the electricity on Guemes Island. Tom Halle was captain and I was the mate. We were crossing Rosario Strait for Guemes Channel with a log tow. Rosario Strait, Bellingham Channel and Guemes Channel all converge in the same area, with each one's current on a different time schedule. With a log tow that can make only 2 knots and a current that can get up to 4 or 5 knots the timing has to be just right to navigate across the stretch of water from Thatcher Pass to Guemes Channel.

As we approached Guemes Channel the current was changing from ebb to flood. The current in Bellingham Channel was still running out and the current in Guemes channel was starting to run in. We were at the north side of the entrance to Guemes Channel and as the current changed we started in. We had been facing north into the current and began our transition to the east for Guemes Channel. The current began to push us sideways. Before we could straighten out, the stern of the log tow ran over a navigation buoy which became tangled in the tow and we were dragging it up the channel. Before the buoy popped back out of the tow it cut the underwater power cable that supplies Guemes Island with electricity. We both had been in the wheelhouse as we approached that buoy and had discussed how best to pass it. I had suggested the north side. That didn't work out too well but of course the captain takes all the blame.

Several years later I was telling that story to a gentleman at a dinner party. When I mentioned Guemes Island his face lit up and he pointed a finger at me and said, "Aha! That was you! I had to fix that mess." He said he had spent three days without much sleep leasing a tug and barge and getting a crew together, to fix our foul-up. We all had a good laugh over that.

Tugboat Life (1959 to 1969)
Chapter 20
I make Captain: Barge Rollover

We were at the dock in Anacortes awaiting the discharge of our loaded gravel barge in the fall of 1969 when I got the word to pack my bag; a replacement was coming for me. An old friend of mine, Larry Jensen, arrived to take over as mate. Larry had just been rehired after two years working as a ground spotter/flagger for a local crop-duster. Larry also brought word that I was to report back to the company office. Oh boy what now? When I arrived at the office in La Conner I was ushered into President James Dunlap's office. He explained to me that the company was adding more crews and he would like me to take over as captain on the tug *Crosmor*.

Malolo (left) **and the** *Crosmor (right)*

The *Crosmor* was a single screw fifty foot tug powered by a Caterpillar diesel engine. The crew's quarters were at the front of the main deckhouse with two bunks on each side. The captain's cabin was on the upper deck behind the wheelhouse. After explaining a few more things he suddenly stopped. He then said, "You do want the job don't you?" I said, "Yes." I knew this could happen some time in the future, but it was still a shock. My first thought was, "I've got to go home and tell my wife." When I got home and told her the news she was excited for me and gave my dad a call. We saw him later the same day and he called me Captain Bell; that would take some getting used to. I was 29 years old.

My new crew consisted of a very experienced mate, Duane (Red) Bretvick; a tall, slim easy going guy, with red hair, who everybody liked. The rest of the crew included two deckhands; Harvey Anderson and Bob Lynch. Harvey was a classmate from high school that I had just talked into coming to work for Dunlap. Bob Lynch was a young full of energy guy just out of school who had been recently hired.

Our first job, as a new crew on the tug *Crosmor*, was a log tow from West Sound on Orcas Island to Sidney, B.C. We departed West Sound even though we had an extremely bad forecast of gale warnings for the next morning. Even with the bad weather approaching I decided to get underway. My plan was to work my way to the south in Haro Strait then cross to the islands on the west side and head north to Sidney Harbor. If the wind started to blow I would have it on my stern and be less vulnerable to damage.

As the morning passed and I studied the chart I realized that the area where I planned to make my crossing was strewn with submerged rocks. If the wind came up during the crossing I might have trouble navigating through those obstacles. I finally abandoned plan A and headed back north towards deeper water. By the time I cleared the rock strewn area and turned west the south wind had started to blow. The side of the tow was exposed to the wind and taking a beating. About this time a Washington state ferry was going by and called us on the VHF radio. The ferry captain asked if he needed to slow down to decrease his wake, and then said, "What are you guys doing out here in all this wind." I said, "I wish we weren't here, but since we are I have my fingers crossed and am hoping for the best."

By slowing down and pulling gently on the tow we managed to make it into calm waters, after two or three hours, with the loss of only a couple logs. After delivering the tow in Sidney we went to the city dock for customs and I called our dispatcher in La Conner. His comment was, "Wow! You're there already?" It felt good to hear that but it was only luck that the tow survived and I realized I had been a little too gung-ho and should have waited until the next day after the storm had passed.

We had another incident later on, in which I'm not sure whether more experience would have helped or not. We were dispatched from La Conner to Friday Harbor to pick up a barge loaded with gravel and a new Caterpillar front loader for delivery to Cherry Point Refinery near Ferndale. The barge was loaded with crushed rock. It was January and the temperature was in the low twenties when we got underway. The mate was on watch and I had gone to bed. At about two in the morning I got a wake up call from the mate who casually said, "The barge has just rolled over." I jumped out of bed and said, "Are you kidding me?" "No. It rolled over!" I think I uttered some four letter words while trying to understand what had just happened in the past few seconds.

At the north side of Orcas Island the barge had hit a tide rip and took a shear (sharp turn) which caused the barge to lean just enough that the load of icy crushed rock started to slide like marbles which caused a chain reaction. The more it rolled the more the gravel slid and it went right over dumping nine hundred ton of gravel and a brand new front loading Caterpillar to the bottom in about 360 feet of water.

The mate had a spot light on the barge when it rolled so he took the boat out of gear and at that point the tow bridles fell off the upside-down barge. So we had an upside-down barge and the bridles had fallen off. We lucked out that there were two pad eyes on the bottom of the barge near the bow for us to hook to.

With the loaded barge we could have made about six or seven knots but upside down we could only make two knots. It was decided to take the barge to Seattle where a crane could roll it back upright. The front loader and the gravel were a total loss.

On our way to Seattle we passed through the Swinomish Channel and had to stop at La Conner to wait for high tide. We tied the barge up and went to our home dock. In the office, after explaining what had happened that morning, the only thing James Dunlap said to me was, "Don't wait too long to leave and miss the tide." Another person made the comment that we probably shouldn't have towed the barge if it was overloaded.

The barge had been loaded and left at a mooring buoy by another tug crew. This had been a freak accident caused by extreme cold weather conditions so we didn't think our jobs were in jeopardy.

Tugboat Life (1959 to 1969)
Chapter 21
Moving to *Kiket*: Start Building New Barges

My five man crew had been created to tow freight barges. For log and gravel barge towing, a four man crew was used. The fifth man added was a cook. On a four man crew the lowest senior man did the cooking. The mate and the two deckhands were the primary cargo handlers while the captain and the cook drove the boat underway and the cook prepared three meals a day. The captain and the cook also helped with the cargo after getting enough sleep.

At the beginning, our time was split between freight barging and log towing. Dunlap towing and Puget Sound Freight Lines then joined together to form a company called Merchants Transportation. Dunlap supplied the tugs and crews and Puget Sound provided the barges and the business. To start, we towed decommissioned freight boats. At the same time Dunlap and Puget Sound started building covered barges. The first built was the *Swinomish*, followed by the *Skagit* and the *Dungeness*. These barges were all the same size, 150 feet long, 50 feet wide with a 22 foot high covered house and could carry 1200 ton of cargo. Fully loaded they would draw (sink down in the water) ten feet compared to three feet empty. The hulls were steel and the house was a steel frame covered with corrugated aluminum siding on top of a four foot solid steel wall. They had a 20 foot wide roll-open door on the starboard side and a roll-back roof, the same width as the door, which opened up half the width of the roof.

Tug *Kiket* and barge *Dungeness* at Citizens Dock (Bellingham, WA.)

Unlike the old freight boats that had elevators to load cargo these new barges used forklifts with extending masts to pick the cargo off the dock. Puget Sound Freight Lines continued to build barges over the years and ended up with seven. The next two were the *Tumwater* and the *Whidbey*, each 190 feet by 60 feet with an 1800 ton capacity. After that came the *Barkley Sound*, 225 feet with 2500 ton capacity, and the *Cape Flattery,* 265 feet with a whopping 3000 ton capacity.

In 1970 our crew was assigned to a bigger tug. Dunlap Towing purchased the tug *Elmore* from American Tow Boat Company of Everett, Washington. The *Elmore* was a 60 foot wooden tug with a direct-drive reversing diesel engine. Since a direct reversal engine has no reverse gear, the engine had to be stopped, and the cam shifted so the engine will then run in reverse. This is all accomplished with two levers in the wheel house that are attached to the engine with small cables that run through a series of pullies down to the engine. Air pressure did the starting and the shifting of the cam. This system had about six shifts before it ran out of air, then it was dead in the water for five minutes while the pressure built back up again. This worked okay for log towing but it created a problem when handling barges.

My crew on the *Crosmor* and I were chosen to be one of the two crews to run this new addition to the company. Gene Dunlap was the company founder. He lived on Kiket Island just east of Deception Pass in Similk Bay so the name of the new tug was changed from *Elmore* to *Kiket*.

A day of orientation on the *Kiket* had been scheduled by our office but I had other obligations and was unable to attend. This was to be a two crew boat and Darrel Bassford's crew would do the first crew up. Our first crew up was scheduled for midnight at the Puget Sound Freight Lines warehouse just north of the Rainbow Bridge in La Conner. To say the least I was a little apprehensive. I had yet to handle this tug with its unfamiliar operating system. To make matters worse it was dark and raining and the tide was running at a pretty good clip to the north. As it turned out the barge loading was not complete and my crew would have several more hours of work before we could depart. I went to bed and when I was awakened just after daylight the wind and rain had stopped and the tide was slack. I couldn't believe my luck. We got underway without any problem with one of the new covered barges for Rayonier Mill in Port Angeles with a load of baled wood pulp.

**Three of Puget Sound Freight Lines newer barges
(Notice that the *Barkley Sound* and the *Cape Flattery* have doors that slide up above the house on a 45 degree angled frame and the *Whidbey* has a door that slides open along the side of the house.)**

Tugboat Life (1959 to 1969)
Chapter 22
Crew on *Kiket*: Ship and barge Collision

My five man crew on the *Kiket* consisted of three inexperienced crew members plus the mate and myself. My experience as a captain was limited to log towing and gravel barging. When we landed gravel barges we did the landings on the tow wire. When landing a barge on the tow wire we shortened the wire until the tug's stern was almost tight against the bow of the barge. Crew members boarded the barge then we continued on until we were at our mooring position. Lines were secured from the barge's bow to the dock and then I backed in against the barge forcing it to lay flat against the dock where it would be further secured.

We used this same procedure with cargo barges in the beginning. After securing the barge, three crew members began either loading or unloading cargo. The cook and myself went to bed or helped with cargo, depending on our need for sleep.

As time went by business was increasing and we were spending all of our time hauling cargo barges. Interstate 5 was being built at this time and trucks soon began taking over the hauling of small consumer goods and canned food. As a result we would transition into hauling pulp, paper and some lumber. From the time that the first settlers arrived in Puget Sound, cargo and passengers were being hauled over water. As the roads were built there was a slow shift to land transportation. Just as the steam powered paddle wheelers had given way to the diesel powered, propeller driven vessels, we were replacing the cargo ships with our barge operation.

We were working two weeks on and two weeks off and as a low seniority, just recently promoted captain, I was making higher wages (because of the cargo handling in addition to captain's wages) than the other captains at Dunlap. It was decided that we would rotate jobs. One month on freight hauling, then one month log towing.

The first two week period that we changed jobs the captain that replaced me on the *Kiket* had a very exciting time. They were towing up the Fraser River with a full load of wood pulp when they ran into thick fog. This was before we had radar. They saw a buoy at a bend in the river and realized they were on the wrong side of the channel, just as they heard a fog horn of a ship coming down river. They headed across to the proper side. As they reached the other side and with the barge still hanging out in the channel a large Russian freighter came barreling through the fog. The bow of the tug was about to run aground on the beach and the freighter was swinging wide with the barge still in the channel. The ship hit the stern port corner of the barge. The bow of the ship sliced off about three feet of a triangle shaped piece of the barge's hull and the flair of the ship's bow crunched in a portion of the upper house of the barge. The damage was all above the waterline so the barge stayed afloat.

When the ship hit the barge the Russian captain asked the pilot, "What was the nationality of the barge?" The pilot told him American and the Russian said, "no-no-no not American," with a heavy Russian accent. This was during the Vietnam War. This incident eventually went to a Coast Guard hearing and the pilot of the ship that hit the barge got most of the blame because of traveling at too high a speed in the fog. The rotation plan did not last too much longer and I settled in to full time on the *Kike*t.

In the early summer of 1970 another big change in my sailing life came along. We were told that Dunlap Towing and Puget Sound Freight Lines would be splitting apart and that we could choose which company we stayed with. This turned out to be a tough decision for me and I imagine for others. I felt a strong loyalty towards Dunlap Towing because they had hired me for my first real job. I had been with them for 10 years. On the other hand, I was the captain on the tug *Kiket* and it would be going to Puget Sound Freight Lines. At Puget Sound the pay would be higher because of the cargo handling that was paid in addition to tugboat pay wages.

Management in both companies had agreed not to try to influence our decision. Both companies made it clear that they wanted me to choose them. The higher wages and the uncertainty of what I would be doing if

I stayed with Dunlap won me over and I decided to go with Puget Sound Freight Lines.

It had been 10 years since I first started work on tugs. In my second year I was being used on a few short trips as captain. Then the Army took me away for 2 years and when I came back to work business was slow and I had to stay as mate for the next 4 years before I got a full time captain's job.

PART – II
Tugboat Life (1970 to 1998)
Chapter 23
Starting Puget Sound Freight Lines: Sinking of La *Conte*

On July 1, 1970 the transition was made from Dunlap Towing to Puget Sound Freight Lines. It included two tugs (the *Kiket* and the *Narada*) some of the Dunlap employees and some new hires to include four crews, a total of twenty people.

The *Kiket* had a long history. Her keel was laid in 1889 when she was named *R.P. Elmore* and was launched in 1890. She had a wood hull, and was a steam powered passenger vessel working between Astoria and Tillamook, Oregon. In 1898 a Port Townsend business man purchased her and used her to haul passengers and freight to Alaska for the Klondike gold rush. In 1901 she became the property of American Tug Boat Company. In 1922 a fire burned her to the waterline and she was rebuilt as a tugboat and fish hauler and renamed just *Elmore*. Her steam engine was replaced at that time with a 110-horsepower three cylinder diesel engine built by Washington Iron Works. Two more engine replacements occurred over time, a 6 cylinder Washington Iron Works direct reversal engine that was in her when purchased by Dunlap towing in 1969. Then Puget Sound Freight Lines replaced that engine with a modern Caterpillar diesel engine during a remodel in 1970.

The *Narada* was owned by Puget Sound Freight Lines. She had started her life as a fishtender, and then was used as a tugboat. She was a 66 ton, 77 foot vessel built in 1919 with a double-planked oak hull and a 365 horsepower diesel engine. Puget Sound Freight Lines sold her in the early 1970s and her new owner converted it back into a fishing vessel and renamed her *La Conte*. The *La Conte* sank on January 30, 1998, in the Gulf of Alaska during a monster storm with the loss of two lives. Two books have been written about the rescue of the crew and are titled *Coming Back Alive* and *The Last Run*.

One day we were being dispatched from La Conner by Dunlap Towing. The next day it was from Puget Sound Freight Lines in Seattle. Puget Sound Freight Lines headquarters was at Pier 62 in Seattle. Pier 62 and 63 warehouses were used for general freight and Pier 66 for pulp and paper products. Puget Sound Freight Lines had four warehouses in Tacoma that were used to discharge incoming freight that was shipped out from there by either truck or rail. They also had warehouses in Olympia, La Conner and Bellingham. Besides moving freight to and from these docks we would soon be hauling in cargo from other ports including Port Townsend, Port Angeles and several Canadian destinations.

We were required to provide our own transportation to Pier 62 in Seattle our home port. Puget Sound Freight Lines provided transportation for crew changes at other destinations. My crew on the *Kiket* was all from Skagit Valley. I volunteered to transport everybody on the crew to Seattle so I needed a larger car. One of my neighbors had a 1959 Oldsmobile 88 four door sedan for sale for $400.00. It was good solid transportation for our five man crew. I picked up each person at his house and deliver him back at the end of our two week shift.

THE SINKING OF THE *La CONTE* [6]

The sinking of the *La Conte*, formerly the *Narada*, occurred on the Fairweather Grounds, 150 miles north of Sitka in the Gulf of Alaska. The crew of fishermen arrived on the grounds on January 25, 1998, and set out their longlines to start fishing for cod. A longline is a line of several hundred feet and every few feet has an attached short line with a hook on it. The hooks are baited and the longline is anchored at each end with a buoy line running up to the surface. The weather had started to deteriorate so the captain decided to leave some of the long lines in the water and headed for safe port 80 miles to the southeast at Graves Harbor. They spent two days waiting out the weather in Graves Harbor.

The weather forecast was still not good when they arrived back out on the grounds to retrieve their fish and gear on January 30th. The hooks were loaded with fish so they worked all day pulling in their catch. The weather was not looking good and some of the experienced crewmen were questioning the decision

---

[6] This story is collected from information in book *Coming Back Alive (Author Spike Walker published by St Martin's Press)*, and a series in the Juneau *Empire*, Juneau Alaska, December 20-24, 1998 by Todd Lewan.

to stay out with conditions deteriorating. The need for a large payday influenced the captain to stay at it longer than he should have.

By evening, when they were headed back to port after retrieving their gear, they were into a full blown storm with hurricane force winds. The old wood planked vessel started taking on water faster than the onboard pumps could get rid of it. Water came up and shorted out their pumps so they tried bailing with buckets but couldn't keep up. The engine soon died and they were drifting at the mercy of the storm and monstrous waves. They sent out a mayday call and got on survival suits. Next a huge swell hit the stern, blew out all the windows and rolled her over on her side. She soon righted herself but they knew they were in big trouble so the captain got them together to abandon ship. He tied them together with a line and tied the EPIRB to the line. The EPIRB is an emergency radio beacon that will transmit a signal to a satellite that relays the signal to a command control center in Washington, DC. On the captain's command they all five tied themselves together jumped into the darkness not knowing if the water was 10 feet or 100 feet down.

A computer at the Washington, DC center had received the information from the satellite and transferred it to the US Coast Guard Station at Juneau, Alaska. The EPIRB could have identified the vessel but it hadn't been registered. A half hour passed while the Coast Guard broadcast to all ships in the area to see if anyone had accidentally triggered their EPIRB. A 200 pound man in a survival suit had an 83%

chance of surviving 2.7 hrs in the 38 degree water, which dropped to 51% in 4.7 hours.

A helicopter was dispatched from Sitka but they had no idea what the emergency was, because the buoy was not registered. They had no way of knowing if any one was in the water. Out at the Fairweather Grounds the men in the water were being pummeled by 80 foot seas. Each time they were buried under tons of water and came up coughing and throwing up salt water. After a while they were down to four with one man missing – they continued to call his name with no response.

The helicopter turned on a direction finder and received a weak signal from the EPIRB. They spotted the men with the helicopter flood light reflecting off the reflective tape on their suits. The wind gusted to 120 knots and hovering at 100 feet the swells came within 5 feet of the belly of the helicopter. When they tried to lower the 40 lb rescue basket it set back at a 45 degree angle. Salt water flares were dropped in the water to give the pilot a point of reference. Suddenly one flare disappeared and the pilot thought it had gone behind a wave. He was wrong - it was riding on top of a huge wave *above* the helicopter! The men in the water were also on the top of the wave looking down in horror at the whirling blades of the helicopter below them. The pilot managed to avoid the wave but now he was low on fuel and had to head back to base leaving all the men in the water.

A second helicopter got underway and soon found the men in the water and tried for a rescue but the closest they could get the basket to the men in the water was 30 feet. They too had to head back because of being low on fuel without rescuing any of the men. It had been 5 hours and 45 minutes since the *La Conte* sank.

A third helicopter was underway and had added extra fuel and flares. When they arrived on the scene it took them 20 minutes of fighting the wind and dodging waves to get the basket next to the survivors. One of the men broke away from the group and swam to the basket and climbed aboard. He was quickly hoisted into the helicopter. The basket was lowered again and this time landed 10 yards from the survivors. Because of the snow and spray they were unable to see if they had anyone in the basket but the cable came tight so they pulled it up. As the basket came up to the door they tried to pull it in but it wouldn't budge so they pulled harder and then saw that a second man was clinging to the bottom of the basket. Just as they saw him, he dropped loose and fell back into the sea. The altimeter read 103 feet - that's a long way to fall! The man just rescued told them that the man that dropped back into the water was the captain. Another man was spotted near a strobe light and was soon in the helicopter. They searched until they spotted a fourth man but when they dropped the basket next too him he showed no sign of motion. They bumped him with the basket but there was no response. The fuel gauge indicated it was time to leave so they headed back to base with three survivors.

The next morning at daylight rescue planes were sent out and they found one body, but the fifth man could not be found. Seven months later two teenage boys were deer hunting on Shuyak Island, 650 miles to the north near Kodiak Island. No humans lived on this island. As they were hiking along a bear trail they came upon part of a glove from a survival suit with a decomposed human hand in it. On further investigation they found a bear bed near by with the upper part of the survival suit in it. They reported it to the authorities and an investigation revealed that it had come from the *La Conte*. The Gulf of Alaska had swept the body all that way and washed it up on the beach were it was found by a black bear wandering along the beach.

Because I knew the *La Conte* in the early days when it was used as a tug, I felt especially bad when I heard about its terrible end and the loss of two crew members. The sea can be VERY unforgiving!

Tugboat Life (1970 to 1998)
Chapter 24
Landing Barges with Tug Alongside

I felt that with my "green" (inexperienced) crew and starting a new business, hauling freight with a tug and barge, we needed to refine our procedures. The change I had in mind was not landing our barges on the tow wire, it was instead landing them with the tug alongside. This process was called "flopping on the barge" or "hipping up to the barge." One of my crew members had heard a management person mention that they hoped I would stop using tow line landing. It was time to change the way of doing things.

By taking the barge alongside the tug we had more control and were less likely to damage the dock. Most of the crew had never seen this maneuver performed. My introduction to this method came when I was a deckhand on the tug *Vulcan*. The captain, the mate and I, were in the wheelhouse as we were about to take a barge alongside. They asked me to go on deck and get the springline ready. My pride kept me from asking what that was and I went out to take a look, thinking it would be obvious. Not being able to find anything that looked like a coil spring I looked back at the wheelhouse and saw the captain and mate cracking up with laughter. I realized I had been had. The "springline" is the name used for one of the three mooring lines used to take a barge alongside. I had a lot to learn.

My first try at this procedure occurred in Bellingham. I explained to the crew what we were going to do as we approached the waterway. The hookup and landing went smoothly. Harvey Anderson was the mate on the barge with the radio and said afterwards "that was easy. It went so smooth."

The procedure included pulling in the tow wire until the barge was right on the stern of the tug. Then positioning the tug at about a 45 degree angle to the barge and letting the barge run into the stern of the tug. The momentum of the barge would fold the boat around until it was lying parallel with the barge. Three lines would be attached, a springline, sternline and a bowline. The lines were drawn tight with the use of a bow windless, stern winch, or a capstan depending on the tugs configuration.

Later on we used lines fixed in place to streamline the process. Two of the lines were fixed at a set length and the third was used to tighten the "hook-up", the tighter the hook-up the better the maneuverability. This was for pushing the barge backwards. To push forward we unhooked from the barge, moved to the stern of the barge and attached to it with the same three line hook-up. Unhooking from the barge could be quite risky if the wind was blowing. Our new covered barges with their large deck house could be easily pushed by the wind. We developed a process of letting the tow wire fall off the side of the tug and letting the barge coast on by, then hooking up to the stern. After the lines were attached to the barge the tow wire was pulled tight underneath it. Departure was easy also because you were already hooked-up.

With the barge alongside and the lines tight the crew went aboard the barge to prepare for the landing. Being alongside a barge with a large deckhouse I could only see my side of the barge – so, the mate used a CB radio to guide me to the dock. The mate would either give me rudder and throttle commands or he would give me the distance and angle of approach and I would make the necessary executions.

At Puget Sound Freight Lines we developed a procedure of approaching the dock at about a forty five degree angle. The mate gave the distance to the dock and the correct angle of approach. When the bow came within a few feet of the dock the mate gave the command to back the tug which pulled the bow of the barge away, shifted it parallel to the dock, and slowed it down. We settled gently against the mooring and slid into position with a sternline that was used to stop us in the right spot.

Some companies required their captains to be on the barge and take control of the landings. At Puget Sound Freight Lines our crews tended to stay together, sometimes for years, and we developed a well coordinated team with everybody able to do their job without supervision.

Tugboat Life (1970 to 1998)
Chapter 25
Tug Crew: Remodeling of *Kiket*: Start Building Tugs

My crew on the *Kiket* when we started with Puget Sound Freight Lines was Duane Bretvick, Harvey Anderson, John Olson and Bob Lynch.

Duane Bretvick, who everybody called Red, lived with his family in La Conner. Locally, Red fished the Skagit River as a commercial fisherman but had switched to tug boating when the fishing no longer produced a profitable living. On the *Kiket's* crew Red and I were the only ones with experience in the beginning. Red had been a captain at Dunlap Towing for a while in the mid 1960s. The towing business had slowed down and he had gone back to a mate's position. He had been offered the same captain's job that I had but had turned it down leaving me the opportunity. Red was an easy going guy that everybody liked and was very competent in doing his job. This sure made my job easier as a new captain.

I had graduated from La Conner High School with Harvey Anderson and he had gone on to college and then into the Army at the beginning of the Vietnam War. After being discharged from the Army in the mid sixties he got a job at Boeing. He was laid off from Boeing during a slow down in business and was working at his dad's service station in La Conner when I talked him into trying towboating. Harvey was well acquainted with boats and working around the water. His dad's service station had a small boat service on the waterfront in La Conner.

John was not too long out of school and still living at home when he was hired by Puget Sound Freight Lines when we switched over from Dunlap. Bob was about the same age as John and was married; they both lived in the Mount Vernon area.

We got along very well together as a crew. Life on a tugboat can be very good or very bad depending on the people you work with. We carpooled together to and from Skagit Valley to Seattle. This did not last long. The company was growing and in a couple of years, Red moved into a captains job and Harvey took over as mate. In those days captains and mates were not required to have a Coast Guard license. In the mid 1970s the Coast Guard changed this requirement and all captains and mates had to take a short Coast Guard test and were issued a "Not More Than 200 Gross Ton Near Coastal Operators License."

When Puget Sound Freight Lines started up they decided to remodel the *Kiket* with a new wheelhouse, galley and main engine, so we were moved to the *Narada* during this process. At about the same time they started building new boats. The first to be built in 1970 was the *Edith Lovejoy,* named for the wife of one of the founders. The *Edith Lovejoy* was a 70 foot steel hull, single propeller tug with an 1100 horse power Caterpillar diesel main engine. As soon as the *Edith* was finished they started building the *Anne*

Carlander. She was finished in May of 1972 and was named after another one of the company founder's relatives and was almost an exact copy of the *Edith Lovejoy*. The difference being that the *Anne Carlander* had a bow-thruster and a larger fuel capacity, 13,000 gallons for the *Edith* and 19,000 gallons for the *Anne*. Both were equipped with Kort nozzles, a large metal hoop that wrapped around the seven foot propeller and created a jetlike effect in the water that added about 10 percent horsepower. They had no rudder. The nozzle could be rotated from side to side to do the steering. These two tugs turned out to be very nice, quiet, modern tugs and are still in use today in British Columbia, Canada.

Tug ***Kiket***

Tug *Anne Carlander*

Anne Carlander with loaded cargo barge in tow.

A view of steerable Kort nozzle

Steerable Kort nozzle

Tug Boat Life (1970 to 1998)
Chapter 26
Wind Storm Seattle Harbor, Port Townsend and Port Angeles, Wind at Discovery Bay

In 1970 when we had just started with Puget Sound Freight Lines, Hugh Marsh was dispatcher and had recently been promoted to the position. We received written orders from Hugh for two days or up to two weeks. Hugh lived in Snohomish and we checked with him daily at the office and at home on weekends. The office was located at pier 62 on the Seattle waterfront. Pier 62 was one of a group of finger piers extending into Elliott Bay along the Seattle water front. The lower portion was warehouse and above the offices of Puget Sound Freight Lines. There was one large open space with five or six desks scattered around for the staff, and four separate offices for management.

On one Sunday we were headed into Seattle on the tug *Narada* with a loaded barge for Pier 62 and as we approached Elliot Bay the wind started to blow a gale from the southwest, and the swell was starting to build up. I soon realized that there was too much wind and swell to make our landing. The swell was sweeping across Elliott Bay and crashing into the docks along the waterfront. I called Hugh Marsh and told him we would be going to the West Seattle buoy to wait out the weather. I could tell from his voice that he was having trouble believing this. We continued on to the buoy and had quite a battle getting tied up. As we pulled up to the buoy and slowed down to shorten the tow wire the wind (blowing about 50 knots) blew us backwards and we had to stop and pull back to the buoy. This took several tries. The *Narada* had about 400 HP and the winch pulled the wire in only at an idle. At an idle the wind blew the bow of the tug around and we had to stop pulling wire and speed up to straighten the bow back into the wind. When we finally got tied to the buoy we had to wait about 6 hours until the wind died down and we were finally able to make our landing. Hugh Marsh later told me that he couldn't believe that the conditions were so bad that we couldn't get into the dock. So he drove the 50 or so miles from Snohomish to Seattle on a Sunday morning to check for himself. Upon his arrival at Pier 62 it was high tide and the waves were washing right up on the dock. I think this was the last time he questioned a captain's judgment. It was the beginning of a trusting and cordial relationship that lasted over twenty years.

Our group of "country-boy tugboaters" were still getting used to the big city company and building trust between us. A landing we made at Pier 62 may have helped build that trust. We were on the tug *Narada* with one of the covered barges alongside approaching Pier 62. Coming downwind with about 30 knots on our tail, we were approaching the pier at a 90 degree angle. The office crew had a clear view of us through the windows. The president of the company, Howard Lovejoy, told us later that he told everybody to hang on because he thought we were going to crash. As we got closer, with Red on the barge with the radio and me in the wheelhouse, Red told me to, "Let her drift and stand by to back down.." The *Narada's* engine had a tendency to die at an idle so I was a little nervous and kept revving the engine in idle to make sure it was still running. Then I heard Red say, "Back her down full." The boat shuddered and vibrated and the black smoke rolled out. The propeller caught hold of the water and the bow of the barge swung to the right and we settled in against the dock as soft as a feather, much to the surprise of the people upstairs in the office!

Puget Sound Freight Lines won a contract away from Black Ball Line in the early 1970s to haul freight from Port Angeles and Port Townsend to Seattle and Tacoma. This run was Monday, Wednesday and Friday for the Crown Zellerbach Mills. The schedule was an 0800 AM arrival at the Crown Z Mill in Port Angeles for a load of newsprint paper rolls and a stop at the mill in Port Townsend on the way back south if there was space available for wood pulp of various types. This contract also included hauling wood pulp out of the Rayonier Pulp Mill in Port Angeles one or two times a week. The Rayonier shipments went to various places: Seattle, Tacoma, La Conner and Victoria, British Columbia.

Our stay on the *Narada* lasted a couple of months until the *Kiket* was finished with her remodel. During our short stay on the *Narada* we had another trip that stands out in my memory. It was from Seattle to Port Angeles for a 0800 start at Crown Zellerbach. I was on watch alone while the rest of the crew was in bed. Approaching the Port Townsend area the wind was blowing thirty-five knots southeast so I started to hug the shore toward Discovery Bay. As I approached the entrance to Discovery Bay (west of Port Townsend) the wind was blowing seventy knots out through the entrance of the bay. I was crossing at a ninety degree angle to the wind and the empty barge was hanging downwind at a forty degree angle while the boat listed over at about thirty degrees. This woke up Harvey Anderson who was still fairly new at this business and he came into the wheelhouse with a, "What the heck is going on?" look on his face. This white knuckle crossing of the entrance to Discovery Bay lasted only thirty to forty-five minutes. The wind then dropped to about thirty-five knots and the rest of the trip was fairly smooth with the wind on our tail around Dungeness Spit and out to Port Angeles.

When the *Kiket* came back to us she had a new galley, wheelhouse and a new Caterpillar diesel engine. Not too long after that the first of the new tugs that were being built was launched and christened the *Edith Lovejoy*. These new tugs being built were quite different from the old wooden tugs we were used to. They had a wider beam, higher bows, a higher bull rail around the edge of the deck. The inside crew area was modern and the noise level was low, in the low fifty decibels range about the same noise you get riding in a car, It was just as quiet in the staterooms and wheelhouse. One thing that seemed strange was there were no seats in the wheelhouse and no autopilot. The steering was with a manual steering wheel. It took a couple of years to convince management that an autopilot would save fuel.

We got our first look at the new tug *Edith Lovejoy* at Pier 62 in Seattle on a sunny afternoon. I have to admit I was a little jealous of the other crew on the new boat but it may have just been the new company hats they were all wearing. This was the beginning of a fairly rapid company expansion to four tugs and seven barges in the next several years.

Tugboat Life (1970 to 1998)
Chapter 27
Cooks on Tugs

Food quality and cooking expertise varied on the different tugs. At Dunlap Towing, prior to the company going union, the cook on the crew was the lowest senior man or the last man hired. The food was purchased at a local grocery store usually by the captain or the cook and charged to the company account. There were very few restrictions on purchases and it was the captain's responsibility to keep the cost under control. On the "expertise" side it varied from cooks who had experience at restaurant cooking to young deckhands with no experience whatsoever.

One day on the harbor tug *Martha* while pulling a log tow through the Swinomish Channel the captain asked the young deckhand to cook a meal. He went down to the galley and turned on the gas oven then went looking for a match. Unable to find one in the galley he went up to the wheelhouse. The wheelhouse had several people in it and he was quite bashful so he stood there for a while before he asked if anybody had a match. After being handed a box of matches he went back down to the galley and bent down over the oven. He struck the match on the side of the matchbox and the oven blew up in his face. The people in the wheelhouse herd a loud "whoomp" sound from below and in a short time the deckhand came back to the wheelhouse. His face was red and his eyebrows were burnt off but he was not seriously hurt.

A cook/deckhand that was with us for a short while had come to work with a venereal disease and one of the crew members had walked in on him washing his private parts in the bathroom sink. That was the end of his tug boating career.

On four man crews the deckhands did the cooking and on five man crews we had full time cooks who served three meals a day. The food onboard was always available for every one at any time for snacks or a do-it-yourself meal. At Puget Sound Freight Lines I had the same cook for several years. Jerry Thomas had worked on Puget Sound's freight boats, and had transferred on to the tugs when we started the tug and barge operation. He had a master's license but preferred to work in the galley. He could cook the meals, work the deck, drive a forklift or drive the boat. He could do it all well.

From the early 1970s for the next ten years Jerry was the cook, life became fairly routine for him. He served three meals a day worked twelve hours a day and helped with cargo work in-between meals when at the dock. When underway Jerry was up at 0530, and I could just about set my clock by that.

I was alone in the wheelhouse in the winter time, and with it being still very dark at 0530, I was probably kind of bored so I played a few practical jokes on Jerry. One morning I hid in a dark corner when Jerry came into the wheelhouse with his morning cup of coffee. He sat down and looked around wondering where I was. I let this go on for a few minutes before I jumped out to try to scare him.

Some of the crew members sometimes volunteered to do the cooking. This was usually when we were tied to a dock and performing no cargo work. Ken Miller, a mate, could make a "Killer Seafood Chowder" that was out of this world delicious!

When the schedule allowed, we departed Seattle a day early for a trip to either Port Alberni or Gold River on the west coast of Vancouver Island. We would stop before entering either of the inlets and catch a few cod fish then proceed on into the dock where we would have a feast. With the advent of Vessel Traffic Systems keeping an eye we had to be a little more creative about making these stops. We knew where there were blind spots in the radar coverage and would inform the traffic control operator we were slowing down. This would give us time to stop and catch our fish. We ate well. The catch would include rock fish, ling cod and yellow eye. For these occasions a case of beer was purchased in Seattle before departure. For special occasions like Thanksgiving, Christmas or New Years I brought a bottle of rum for before dinner drinks if we were staying overnight at a dock. By the end of the 1970s liquor was no longer allowed on boats. Of course this rule was enacted because of a few people abusing this privilege. Our crew had curtailed drinking prior to this ruling because on one trip when we finally got time to have our evening drink we found our bottle was empty. Somebody had been sneaking liquor and we all pretty well knew the culprit.

At Dunlap Towing, the crew bought the groceries at a local store. At Puget Sound Freight Lines we had order forms to fill out and the groceries were delivered to us by a supplier. At Olympic Tug and Barge, where I later worked, the captain bought the groceries at a Safeway store with a company account. Even later yet, when I moved to Pacific Northwest Marine Services, the captain bought the groceries with a company credit card. Later the company owners delivered the groceries from a list we produced. This change didn't come about because we were abusing the privilege but because the owners wanted to buy from Costco and take advantage of the cash rebate. The amount of money spent depended on the length of the voyage. I've spent as little as $50 and as much as $3000 for a single trip.

Tugboat Life (1970 to 1998)
Chapter 28
Back on *Kiket*: Puget Sound Freight Barging; Storm at Point Wilson

When the *Kiket* came back to us we used it on local runs between Olympia, Tacoma, Seattle, Everett, La Conner, Anacortes and Bellingham. Occasionally we had a run from the Point Wells Oil terminal 15 miles north of Seattle to a fuel dock near Bremerton. They had 30 to 40, 55-gallon barrels of oil sitting on the dock and we had to muscle them on to pallet boards by hand then load them onto the barge with a forklift. Each barge had three forklifts. One was a large heavy duty lifter we would use to lift one of the smaller forklifts up on to the dock. After completing our loading, and retrieving our forklift it was a short two and a half hour hop to Bremerton. Upon arrival we unloaded the pallets of oil and took the barrels off the pallets so we could take them with us. Nobody got much sleep on that "run" the crew worked the whole time.

Another example of a run we made was we started in Olympia where we took on several hundred cases of Olympia Beer on wood pallets. We then went to Seattle where we loaded general cargo, appliances, mattresses, hardware, cases of liquor and empty cans. The cans were in large cardboard boxes, one box per pallet board. The cans were new empties for producing canned salmon and canned vegetables. Next stop would be La Conner to unload empty cans at the fish cannery then shift over to Puget Sound Freight Lines warehouse and unload empty cans and general cargo. After unloading we loaded canned fish and canned vegetables. The next stop was Bellingham to unload general cargo and Olympia Beer, then on to Anacortes to unload empty cans and load canned fish. Finally back to Seattle to unload all cargo. After that we started all over again with a new run.

After Puget Sound Freight Lines took over Black Ball's Olympic Peninsula business in 1971 we started making steady runs to Port Angeles and Port Townsend. Black Ball had been in the freight hauling and ferry business on Puget Sound and Alaska since the early 1800s. We took over the freight business and the State of Washington took over the Ferry business. Black Ball was left with one ferry, running from Port Angeles to Victoria, British Columbia.

Trucks were hauling the smaller freight that we had been handling and we were switching over to the heavier loads of newsprint and wood pulp. The cargo went to Pier 42 in Seattle which had been acquired along with the Black Ball business. These three runs per week out to Port Angeles and Port Townsend provided an easier pace than the harbor-hopping runs around Puget Sound.

Just when things started to get routine along came a nice storm to break up the monotony. This happened on a trip from Everett to Victoria, BC. We departed

Everett early in the morning with a full load of baled wood pulp from Scott Paper Company. The cook took over the wheelhouse and I left instructions for him to give me a call before entering the Straits of Juan de Fuca so I could check the weather. Jerry got me up about 10 AM just as we were passing Point Wilson at Port Townsend and entering the Straits. It was the beginning of a swift running minus ebb tide. I turned on the weather channel on the VHF radio to check the forecast and found out the wind was predicted to be from the west at 50 knots. This was not good. I turned around and headed back toward Point Wilson and sheltered waters. It had been 50 minutes after passing Point Wilson when I made the turn back. It would take us 6 hours back to Point Wilson and calm water. The wind was westerly about 20 knots as we turned and we were facing an increasingly swift, running ebb current. Within a short time the wind was howling out of the west at 50 gusting to 70 knots or higher. The swell built up fast and was soon 15 to 20 feet. We had to slow to an idle to lessen the strain on the tow wire. There were times when I had to take the boat completely out of gear when we were being hit by very large swells as the tow winch rocked back and forth. The possibility was that the winch could be pulled right out of the deck. That would leave a large gaping hole for water to enter. I didn't want to think what could happen after that. Taking the boat out of gear created another problem. The barge would turn sideways to the swell and take a beating from the waves. That was the lesser of two evils; potentially sink the boat or let the barge get beat-up. One thing we had going for us was it was daylight and we could see what was coming at us. One time when looking at the barge, while it was laying sideways to the swell, a large wave hit it and spilled right over the top. The top of the barge is about 25 feet out off the water - that was a big wave! A large ocean-going tug came by with an oil barge in tow and was going completely out of sight behind the biggest swells.

After about 6 hours we were back inside Point Wilson. Here the water was calm and we were sheltered from the wind. We stopped to check our barge. The barge had a 3 foot port list and water was shooting out of a 4 inch scupper like a fire hose. The cargo door had a hole in it we could walk through and water was pooled up about 4 feet deep on the low side of the barge. We were ordered back to Seattle for repairs and to salvage what was left of the cargo. Wood pulp and water do not go well together because it turns the pulp into a consistency of slushy snow. The load sustained about 25 percent damage.

I received a letter from the company president stating that he was glad we had made it through our ordeal. Included was a newspaper article about the storm and that it had blown down 7,000 trees in Moran State Park on Orcas Island.

There were no reprimands or repercussions, but in hindsight there may have been actions I could have taken to avoid that beating. If the cook had awakened me a little earlier my choice might have been different. Or if I had headed for Discovery Bay when I turned around I would have got away from the swift ebb tide and large waves. But once I made my decision and the wind started I was trapped. Just like other aspects in life some decisions you make don't end up so well.

Tugboat Life (1970 to 1998)
Chapter 29
Moving to *Edith Lovejoy*: Freight Boat Captains: Powell River Trips

In 1972 the brand new *Anne Carlander* was launched and christened. This created a shifting around of crews. The crew on the *Edith Lovejoy* moved on to the Anne Carlander, while my crew moved to the *Edith Lovejoy*. This created an opening for new jobs on the tugs. At the same time the company was shutting down its freight boat operation and the positions on the tugs were filled by some of those men.

Two of the former captains on the large freight boats were moved to captain's jobs on the *Kiket*. I was thinking that it had taken me several years to learn the job and how could these guys step in and do this without any experience? Maybe I was a slow learner? Well, I was right. The first captain lasted two weeks then gave up and quit in frustration. He had run over a fishing boat; he had run aground; he caught the tow wire in the propeller; and was having trouble sleeping.

The next captain to take over the *Kiket* lasted a little longer and also had trouble sleeping so had started drinking to settle his nerves. He soon requested to be shifted to a mate's position and was moved to the *Edith Lovejoy* as my mate. The jobs on the big freight boats had been different. They had a large crew which included a helmsman to steer the ship while the captain supervised and gave him directions. On the tug, the captain had more hands-on. The captain did his own steering and there was a barge always following you. The first captain moved on and became a Puget Sound Pilot, the one that moved into a mates position stayed with it until he retired a short time later. I had eased into the captain's job slowly and spent several years as mate observing and occasionally running short runs as temporary captain. Red Bretvick (who had been on with me) moved over to run the *Kiket* and Howard Robbins (who had been running it before this transition) again became captain opposite Red. The lesson learned is that a tug boat captain needs tug boat experience.

On the *Edith Lovejoy,* we made runs to several different pulp and paper mills in Canada. They included the Crofton at Crofton, B.C., 100 miles north of Seattle on Vancouver Island; Port Mellon in Howe Sound, just north of Vancouver, B.C., about 125 miles north of Seattle; Wood Fiber a little further north in Howe Sound; Powell River at Powell River, B.C., 175 miles north of Seattle on the mainland side of the Georgia Strait and Elk Falls just north of Campbell River, B.C., at the beginning of Johnstone Straits, 205 miles north of Seattle. Most of our time was spent traveling between Seattle and Powell River.

Powell River and West View were two small communities sitting side by side at the site of a large MacMillan Bloedel paper mill. They are nestled at the water's edge and surrounded by forest land. The mill produces newsprint in large rolls for export to various newspapers in the western United States. South of the mill was a log storage area that was protected by a row of old cement ships. These ships were built in the United States at the end of World War II when the United States was running low on steel and experimenting with cement. The war ended before these ships could be put to use so they were sold to MacMillan Bloedel for use as a breakwater. The ships came fully provisioned and ready for use right down to the dishes and silverware in the galleys. The rumor was that just about every house in town had a supply of dishes, silverware, and blankets from these ships.

From Seattle the trip to Powell River with an empty barge took about 18 to 20 hours. Upon arrival we tied the barge to their dock at the loading door and stood by. In Canada we were not allowed to load our own barges. The loading took three or four shifts. Two eight hour shifts the first day and finished the next day with one or two shifts. When the load was complete and we had the necessary paperwork aboard we headed back to Seattle, a trip of about 20 to 24 hours.

The last 6 hours before arriving in Seattle I did the steering so the crew could rest up for the unloading. After we were secure to the dock and the unloading was underway I went to bed for 6 hours rest. When my rest was complete I went up to the barge to help with the unloading. Most of the time I took over the job of checking damage to the newsprint as it was unloaded. We noted any damage and estimated the extent and who was at fault, the mill or us. Our company paid for any damage we did. We settled into this routine for the next two years.

Tugboat Life (1970 to 1998)
Chapter 30
Predicting Tidal Currents for Travel Route, Swinomish Channel Bridge

The routine trips to Powell River were occasionally changed to other destinations and sometimes bad weather interfered with our routine. In these cases we had different routes we could travel. They included traveling east of Whidbey Island through Saratoga Passage and Deception Pass or through the Swinomish Channel. A more exposed route took us west of Whidbey Island through Admiralty Inlet and across the Strait of Juan de Fuca then Rosario Strait, San Juan Channel or Haro Strait. After crossing the border into Canada it was up the Strait of Georgia or through the Gulf Islands. If we chose the Gulf Islands we would eventually have to exit into the Strait of Georgia, the large body of water that lies between the south end of Vancouver Island and the mainland.

There are four passes leading out of the islands (from south to north): Active Pass, Porlier Pass, Gabriola Pass and Dodd Narrows. The current in each of these passes could be up to 8 or 9 knots during the fastest running tides. As a general rule anything over 4 or 5 knots of current is more than we wanted to deal with. Along with the weather the tides were important in choosing our route, because on a north bound trip to Powell River I was able to shave 2 to 3 hours off our transit time by hitting the tide right in Admiralty Inlet, Haro Strait and Active Pass.

The current in the Swinomish Channel and Deception Pass are on a different time schedule than the current in most of the surrounding waters. The Swinomish Channel current, on the out-going tide, runs out at both ends in opposite directions then it turns and runs south part way through the tide. The same with the incoming tide; it flows in from both ends then part way through the tide it all runs to the north. The current is also affected by the wind, the barometric pressure and the amount of water flowing out of the Skagit River that lies just south of the south end of the channel. It is possible to work around the Swinomish Channel for many years and still miss predicting the time of the current changes because of these variables.

The Swinomish Channel is fairly shallow and with 13 feet of deep draft on the *Edith Lovejoy* we needed at least an 8 foot tide. When the Army Corps of Engineers began to do less dredging in the 1990s, we started to bump bottom on 8 foot tides. Today in (2012) with no dredging at all, you would probably need a 12 foot tide with that tug.[7]

Deception Pass is affected by some of these same conditions as well as the incoming and outgoing tide on the east side of Whidbey Island through Saratoga Passage. Transiting through Deception Pass needed to be accomplished within one hour of slack water when towing a barge. After that the current is running too fast for a safe passage. Usually I chose Deception

---

[7] Since then it was dredged in 2013

Pass to avoid the west wind in the Strait of Juan de Fuca.

Even with careful planning things can go wrong! One day, against the current, I tried to take a loaded barge heading east bound about one and a half hours after slack water. I managed to get as far as the bridge, (about half way through the pass) before the current stopped me. The hard part was getting back out of that narrow gut. I had to slow down and let the current flush me back out. If I reduced RPM's too quickly the barge would get wild and head for the rocks. With a little patience I was able to back out and continue southbound on the outside of Whidbey Island.

The Swinomish Channel has its own set of potential problems. Entering from the south end there is a submerged rock jetty on the south side for a short way until you reach Goat Island. Beyond that point the submerged jetty is on the north side. Then there is the 'Hole in the Wall'. It is a narrow S turn between rock walls. After the Hole in the Wall you come to La Conner where the channel is narrow with docks and moored vessels close at hand on both sides. After La Conner it's fairly good going for about five miles. Then you come to the Highway 20 Bridge and the railroad bridge. Originally, Highway 20 was a draw span that raised straight up to allow passage. In about 1975 a high rise bridge was built. The passage was not a straight shot; the two sets of bridges are at different angles. I've had some interesting experiences at these bridges over the years.

One dark night we were southbound with a loaded barge and as we approached the bridges the draw bridge operator was not opening even though we had been blowing the bridge signal on the horn, flashing the spot light, and calling him on the radio. The current was running with us. After exiting the railroad bridge the draw bridge still had not opened. These two bridges are basically side by side with just a short distance between. I would not be able to stop because of the current going with me. I had to do something quick! I managed to turn the tug 90 degrees to the direction of travel and by pulling hard I spun the tug and barge around and reversed directions just before the bridge. I had to go back through the railroad bridge and spin around again and pull up to the sheer wall of the railroad bridge. The current had turned the other direction by then so we tied up to the railroad bridge sheer wall. I climbed up the wall and walked over to the highway bridge and climbed the ladder up to the bridge tender's control house. As I opened the door, the bridge tender was standing at attention with the phone to his ear saying, "Yes, Sir! Yes, Sir! Yes, Sir!" I had contacted the Coast Guard by radio to inform them of the problem and they had finally reached the bridge tender by telephone. He didn't have much to say except to apologize for dozing off. He finally opened the bridge and we continued underway!

Years earlier, one of Dunlap's tugs was transiting through the open draw bridge at night when a car failed to stop, ran through the barrier and plunged into the channel in front of them. They were able to rescue the one person that had been in the car.

Old Swinomish Channel draw bridge[8]

---

[8] Wikipedia

Tugboat Life (1970 to 1998)
Chapter 31
Operator License; License Test: Traffic Lanes

Prior to 1972 an operator's license was not required to operate an uninspected tugboat. All tugs under 200 ton are uninspected. But that year it changed and I found myself in Seattle at the US Coast Guard headquarters in a room with about 30 other veteran tugboaters taking our first test for a license. We were all seated on both sides of a long table. The tests were handed out and the test administrator stated that he wanted to run through the questions before we started. He read through each question and commented on each. He may not have given the answers but we got enough information so the answer was very clear. I marked each answer with a lead pencil and when the test started I erased the lead mark and replaced it with ink. I got 100%. All of these men were employed by many different tugboat companies and I don't think they let anybody fail the test. This fulfilled the new law without ignoring experience.

The license I obtained was a US Coast Guard "Operator of Uninspected Towing Vessels Upon Oceans Not More Than 200 Miles Offshore And The Inland Water Of The United States Not Including The Western Rivers Or The Great Lakes." These licenses needed to be renewed every 5 years. I was on the 4th year of issue #8 when I retired. By issue #3, the part about Western Rivers and Great Lakes was no longer included on the license. On issue #4, the "Oceans Not More Than 200 Miles Offshore" changed to "Near Coastal Waters". By the time I renewed Issue #7, some schooling and tests had seeped into the system. Now we were required to test for safety, first aid, and rules of the road. For the first two, I went to schools in Seattle and got my certification.

For "The Rules of the Road," I decided to study at home and go to the Coast Guard to take the test. The

Rules of the Road are rules to determine which vessel has the right-of-away when meeting or passing. Right-of-way is granted according to size, configuration, and ability to maneuver or draft. There are rules for maneuvering in limited visibility. The rules designate lights to display on different types of vessels and daylight shapes to display. There are rules for vessels traveling in or crossing a traffic lane. There are different rules for inland, oceans, rivers, lakes and different parts of the country and the world. And there are more. There are hundreds of questions available for the test. On my first try at the Coast Guard test at Pier 62 in Seattle I missed one too many answers and failed the test. I went back home and studied like mad for a month then went back and took the test again. I missed three too many answers this time. "What the heck is going on?" I started studying again then I got a call from Captain Jeff Rickard. He was having the same problem I was. We both decided to go to the Crawford Sea School at Pier 48 in Seattle. Crawford taught the class and administered the test. We were two guys with 30 years of experience in a room full of beginners. We told lots of sea stories and had lots of laughs and a good time.

For four days, we car pooled to Seattle and at the end of the class on the fourth day we took the test. We both passed each missing only one answer. At the Coast Guard we had 20 questions and could miss 4 and still pass. At the school we got 30 questions and could miss 6 and still pass.
 In 1972 another new regulation was started that affected all boaters on inland waters. It was the "Seattle Vessel Traffic System." The Coast Guard laid

out traffic lanes from Tacoma to the beginning of the Strait of Juan de Fuca and on through Rosario Strait to the Canadian border. Lanes were also extended out through the Strait of Juan de Fuca to the Pacific Ocean. In 1979, a Canadian Traffic System was put in place and the two systems worked together for a smooth transition from one system to the other.

The traffic lanes resemble a freeway with a half-mile inbound lane and an outbound lane the same width with a separation zone one quarter mile wide in-between. Lighted buoys were installed in the areas of a course change. Later on these buoys were fitted with a raycon transmitter that sends out a signal that shows up on radar as a series of dashes and dots which identify each buoy.

The system was voluntary to start with. Before getting underway we called "Seattle Traffic" on VHF radio to report who we were, what we were towing and our destination. After getting underway we made another call giving our speed and our ETA to the next check point among the designated check points throughout the system.

The traffic system's first base of operation was on the second floor at Pier 90 in Seattle. A group of us from Puget Sound Freight Lines went to visit them to see their operation soon after they began. It looked like a scene from an old World War II movie. They had a large table with a layout of Puget Sound on it with little wooden ships for each vessel that was checked into the system.

My first thought was that this was going to be a pain in the hind end but its value soon became apparent for keeping track of vessels in the immediate area and being able to check on conditions, out of the range of reception from other vessels, through the traffic system operators.

Over the years the traffic system would change by adding radar coverage to the entire system with a series of radar towers. Later on GPS came along and Automatic Identification System (AIS) was added to identify all vessels within VHF Radio range, 20 or 30 miles. AIS provide all the information about each vessel, speed, type of vessel, destination, time of closest approach and distance of closest approach to other vessels and more. All this information can be integrated on one screen. I never thought 20 years ago that we would one day be able to see around corners and on the other side of islands. This could never be accomplished by radar but today's technology makes this possible.

Tugboat Life (1970 to 1998)
Chapter 32
Tug *Andrew Foss/Pachena*: Trips to Portland, Oregon

In 1977 Puget Sound Freight Lines bought the tug *Andrew Foss* from the Foss Company. They renamed her *Pachena* for Pachena Point a point of land on Vancouver Island just northwest of the mouth of the Strait of Juan de Fuca.

The *Pachena* had a long history with five different companies. She was built in 1941 at the Jackson Shipyard of Oyster Bay, New York. She started out as the *Dauntless #15* for the Dauntless Towing Company. She was sold to the U.S. Army and renamed *Col. Albert H. Barkley*. After WWII she was bought by Foss and renamed the *Andrew Foss*. She served Puget Sound Freight Lines as the *Pachena* and when they sold her she was renamed *Lumberman*.

Puget Sound Freight Lines had obtained a contract to haul newsprint from a Port Alberni paper mill on the west coast of Vancouver Island to Seattle and needed a larger tug. The *Pachena* was a single screw tug, 107.4 feet long and had 1600 horsepower. Before the *Pachena* was ready to go, Puget Sound Freight Lines hired Foss to haul their barge on the Port Alberni runs. All of the Puget Sound Freight Lines captains took turns riding along with Foss on the *Martha Foss* to get familiar with the territory.

When the *Pachena* was finally ready for service in the spring of 1977, I was transferred to her as captain. My first trip on her was to Port Alberni. We left Seattle early on a nice sunny Sunday morning with one barge in tow. About 15 miles out of Seattle an engine alarm sounded, Wayne Johnson the chief engineer, who had been sitting with me in the wheelhouse, went to check the problem. He came right back and asked me to slow to idle while he did further checking. He was back again in a few minutes and said he had to shut the main engine down because of some kind of problem. I swung the tug out of the way of the barge's path just before the engine died. We were in the area of Edmonds, Washington, where the water is 100 fathoms deep and the wind was calm so there was no danger of the tow wire touching bottom. I called the weekend dispatcher to inform him of our problem and he got another company tug underway from Seattle to come to our rescue. We were towed back to our dock at Pier 7 in Seattle.

The next morning Wayne and I were standing at the edge of the dock when 4 or 5 of the company managers arrived. I was completely ignored as they asked Wayne all of the questions. From my perspective it seemed as if they were trying to prove that he had caused the engine failure. One reason for this may have been that the insurance might pay in full if an employee had caused the problem. Wayne was fairly new in the company and was put to the test but passed with flying colors. It was discovered during the rebuilding that the engine was in bad shape and was already a goner and we just happened to be on it when it died.

The *Pachena* was long and fairly narrow, 25 feet wide, and tended to roll badly in rough weather. She was unique in the fact that the tow winch was in the engine room. The tow wire came through a roller at the back of the deckhouse and down into the engine room. The reason for this may have been because the first tugs built in this class had large steel smokestacks and were top heavy. It was rumored that some had rolled far enough to dip the stack in the water.

Our empty barges were fairly lightweight because they were constructed with large aluminum deck houses. They could be easily blown across the water in the wind. The smaller tugs had no problem when taking a barge alongside while still hooked to the tow wire. But if any of the tugs disconnected from the tow wire they could have a tough time catching it in the wind. While hooked to the tow wire we could just stop the tug and let the barge bump into the stern and it folded us around until we were parallel with the barge. The Pachena was a heavy tug and if we didn't do it just right the barge bumped the stern and stopped. Then there you were, 90 degrees to the barge If I tried to turn (to get alongside the barge) the weight of the tow wire pulled the bow of the barge along and I would be running in circles trying to get parallel. This didn't look very professional.

Another problem with the *Pachena* was the old tug tended to have some leaks inside the wheelhouse in rough weather. The deck in the wheelhouse was steel with a wood grating over it. Often we would end up with 2 or 3 inches of water sloshing around under the grating. It was irritating but not dangerous.

Puget Sound Freight Lines started hauling barge loads of newsprint rolls from Port Alberni to Portland, Oregon, in the late 1970s. We used the tug *Pachena* and towed the barge *Barkley Sound* and later the barge *Cape Flattery*. I made 5 of these long trips, starting in Seattle with an empty barge, out into the Pacific Ocean and into Port Alberni.

After departing Port Alberni on the west side of Vancouver Island and exiting Barkley Sound with the loaded barge, we headed directly for the mouth of the Columbia River. The Columbia River bar at the entrance to the river is famous for its severe sea conditions. Since its discovery in the late 1700s by Europeans it has been estimated there have been 2,000 shipwrecks with a loss of 1,000 lives. It is nicknamed the 'Graveyard of the Pacific'. These conditions are caused by the huge volume of water exiting the river and colliding with the ocean swells. Wind, fog and fast running crosscurrents contribute to the dangerous conditions. The 1,200 miles of the Columbia River and its tributaries drain seven US states and one Canadian province.

We picked up a "bar pilot" at the entrance to the river. The best time for entering the river was at the beginning of the flood tide at the sea buoy off the river's entrance. The flood current pushed us up the river for the next 6 to 8 hours of the 12 hour, 90 mile, trip to Portland. At Astoria, Oregon, the bar pilot got off and a "river pilot" came aboard. With the pilot on board we had a worry-free trip up the river with him advising us of any meeting or overtaking traffic and the best path to take on our way up the river. The trip up the river is scenic, but full of hazards. It's also a well-used waterway with vessels of all sizes from small water craft, large container ships and huge aircraft carriers with everything in between.

As we approached Vancouver, Washington, we turned into the Willamette River and our dock was a short way farther. We landed at Riverside Terminal, a newsprint warehouse. The warehouse was quite amazing. It was completely automated.

The newsprint rolls were stacked on our barge on end and were from 3 ft. to 6 ft tall with up to a ton in weight each. One man on the barge picked up the rolls with a clamp machine and set them on a small flatbed trailer on an elevator at the door of the barge. The clamp machines were forklifts with a set of large clamps that used hydraulic rams to squeeze one or two rolls so they could be picked up and moved. The elevator shifted the trailer up to the dock level where the trailer took off on a rail track and delivered the rolls to the place in the warehouse where they were to be stored. At that destination another man with a clamp machine picked the rolls off of the trailer and stacked them in the proper place. The empty trailer then headed back for another load.

On one of our trips to Portland we traded tugs with another company. Knaption Towing needed a large tug for a trip to Alaska. We received the tug *Washington* in trade. The *Washington* was a twin screw 90 foot tug with about 1200 horsepower. After moving aboard we left for Port Alberni. After we were underway we found out she had some problems. The tow wire was in bad shape but would have to wait until we got to Portland to be changed. I crossed my fingers and hoped and prayed for good weather. The radar was accurate for only 5 miles, and the compass, our only other tool for navigation, had not been checked for accuracy in a long time. As we left Barkley Sound with our loaded barge for the Columbia River I asked the traffic system operator to check my course of travel and his was close to my compass reading. The next morning after going on shift the weather was clear and I was able to spot Cape Disappointment. We were only about 5 miles off our needed course. The weather had held and we had a smooth trip. The bar crossing was calm and the trip up the river was without incident. At Portland we replaced the tow wire and had the compass checked.

The trip down the river took about half the time as the up-river trip. We would have a pilot onboard again and drop him off at Astoria. We timed our exit from the river to go out on the flood tide. The reason for this is the flood current flattens the ocean swell and makes for a smooth ride. On my first trip out of the river the swells were huge. I estimated them to be 40 to 50 feet high. The current stretched them out so the ride was not too bad. It was like rolling over small hills. We had one trip when the weather was too wild to depart the river so we tied up at the port dock at Astoria and waited for a day for the ocean to calm down.

Pachena

Tugboat Life (1970 to 1998)
Chapter 33
Predicting Weather for Alberni Trips

Port Alberni is at the inner end of a 25 mile inlet on the west side of Vancouver Island. The approach is through Barkley Sound that lies 30 miles up the coast from the entrance to the Straits of Juan de Fuca. Barkley Sound is a U shaped inlet on the west side of Vancouver Island. After rounding Cape Beal on the south side of the inlet there is a string of islands paralleling the south shore for 5 or 6 miles! Rounding Cape Beal can be kind of tricky because it is necessary to turn more than 90 degrees and expose the boat and barge to the prevailing southwest swell. You can enter on either side of this string of islands. At the inner end of Barkley Sound there is an entrance to a narrow winding channel for the rest of the way to Port Alberni.

Predicting the weather for our trips to Port Alberni in the late 1970s was not easy. Upon departure from Seattle I never knew what it was like on the ocean end of the Strait of Juan de Fuca. It could be flat calm with no wind at the eastern end of the Strait but with a large, rough swell out at the western end.

If the weather was calm after passing the south end of Vancouver Island then we started feeling a motion from a swell, we knew we might be in for a rough ride

50 miles ahead at the west end of the strait. Even with no wind blowing there still might be a large swell from storms offshore. Waves generated by large storms in the center of the Pacific Ocean can radiate out a long distance.

Normally we traveled north of the traffic lanes along the Vancouver Island shore unless there was a strong southeast wind blowing, then we crossed to the Washington shore.

On one occasion in November at Thanksgiving time we spent 52 hours running back and forth along a five mile stretch of beach on the Washington side east of Neah Bay waiting out the weather. We had tried to anchor on the tow wire by running out several hundred feet of wire in the shallow water of Neah Bay but the high wind had blown us off anchor and we were forced to get underway. The wind was gusting up to 50 knots from the southeast. When we finally headed out into the ocean it was still blowing 25 to 30 knots with heavy rain squalls and we still had a rough ride.

The tide had a big effect on the swell condition. An ebb tide running against the swell caused them to hump up higher and bunch closer together, while the flood tide stretched them out and flattened them. We had 30 miles of open ocean to cross to get into Barkley Sound and back into protected water on our way into Port Alberni.

On trips to Port Alberni we normally had an empty barge with three or four forklifts onboard. The forklifts were parked at the stern of the barge against the bulkhead with their forks on the floor and the brakes on. These forklifts were heavy machines with hard rubber tires. Upon arrival at the dock after a rough ride in the ocean we often found that these machines had moved around a few feet.

Once we had a trip that was so rough that the forklifts had been jumping up and down and left a dent in the steel floor. Then there was a trip that the action was so violent that the masts fell off two forklifts and broke their hydraulic lines, spreading hydraulic oil on the deck. The solution for all this damage was to weld pad eye pockets into the floor (a pocket in the floor with a crossbar) and pad eyes on the back wall of the barge to chain the forklifts to. Now the forklifts were chained down to the deck and back to the wall and the mast on each one was secured so it could not jump free.

When we departed Port Alberni with a loaded barge, we had to be sure how the weather was out on the ocean. Our cargo was newsprint rolls stacked on end on pallet boards, two per board. The rolls were from 30 inches to 55 inches in diameter and up to 6 feet tall. They were stowed in the barge tight against each other up to the ceiling and stair stepped down to one high at the end of the loading. The tug crew then strung heavy cargo straps across the face of the load and used a come-along to make them tight after the longshoremen were through loading.

I had the telephone numbers for all the lighthouses on the west side of Vancouver Island and called the lighthouse keepers to check on the weather. On one trip the barge finished loading in the late afternoon and the weather was not good so I decided to spend the night at the dock and check the weather first thing in the morning. The next morning I called the lighthouse at Amphitrite Point on the north edge of Barkley Sound. The lighthouse keeper said it didn't look good out there and he would not want to go out. The night before a ship loaded with lumber had left Port Alberni. When I called the lighthouse the next morning the tender said the weather was worse and the buoy out in the ocean was being completely buried by the waves and there were three ships in trouble. The next morning the lighthouse tender reported better conditions. The weather was starting to moderate and it would take three hours to reach the ocean so we got underway. The ship that had left two days earlier was limping back into Port Alberni with a bad list to one side. Half of its deckload of lumber was gone and part of what was left was hanging over the side. Ships are not invincible.

Exiting Barkley Sound and entering the ocean around Cape Beal was challenging if large southwest swells were rolling in. The shallow water on the left side extends out 4 miles and then it is only 15 fathoms. To get into deep water we had to travel out 8 miles to the southwest. That could be a long 8 miles if it was rough. The cargo on the barge can't handle heavy sideways rolling. Also by this time we had out 1500 feet of tow wire that can be sagging down 10 to 12 fathoms. The turn to the southeast toward the entrance of the Strait of Juan de Fuca needs to be fairly quick to minimize the amount of time of sideways exposure to the swell. We were always concerned about cargo safety and sometimes pushed those limits until damage occurred just so we knew what it could handle.

Pachena Point
(Between Cape Flattery and Barkley Sound)

Amphitrite Point (North side of Barkley Sound)

Estevan Point (South side of Nootka Sound)

Tugboat Life (1970 to 1998)
Chapter 34
Tug *Duwamish*: Barge *Cape Flattery*: Hawaii Trips

Puget Sound Freight Lines continued to grow and build new barges, so soon they were in need of another tug. An opportunity appeared when the owner of a tug company in Alaska passed away. The equipment was up for sale and included the tugs *Taurus*, *Libra*, *Gemini* and *Mary*. Puget Sound Freight Lines acquired the *Libra* and renamed her *Duwamish*.

A new barge was ready for service at this same time. The *Cape Flattery* and the *Duwamish* were paired together to haul newsprint rolls to Hawaii from Canadian paper mills. Port Alberni, Crofton, Powell River and Elk Falls at Campbell River were the mills shipping paper to Hawaii. Some other items were shipped on these trips as well, such as lumber and some heavy equipment. On the return trips they brought back containers loaded with the personal possessions of military personal and used rental cars.

These trips continued for 8 years before Puget Sound Freight Lines lost the contract. I never made that trip but I heard the stories of their adventures. When crossing the ocean they had to take whatever Mother Nature threw at them. They sometimes headed south down the coast to dodge storms to the north and get the wind on their tail down to the lower latitudes before crossing to Hawaii. On the way back they headed directly for the Strait of Juan de Fuca with the wind at a right angle on their side often making for a rough ride.

On one Hawaiian trip the barge, *Cape Flattery*, which was built with four ballast tanks (tanks that filled with water as needed to stabilize the barge) ran into trouble. When the barge was loaded the ballast tanks were left empty. One tank started taking water off the California coast on a trip to Hawaii with a load of newsprint and the barge listed heavily on the port. The crew was able to get onboard the barge and pump out the tanks enough to limp into San Francisco. The cargo doors on the port side were sealed tight enough that no water got inside the barge and there was no damage to the cargo even though the water was covering part of the door. It was later found that when the barge was built someone had left a large pipe wrench in the ballast piping system and the wrench had worked its way into one of the valves which allowed seawater to back up into the ballast tanks.

The crew of the Duwamish had a two or three day layover in Hawaii while the barge was being unloaded by longshoremen. There were two crews of six men for the *Duwamish*. They changed crews after each one-month trip, working one month on and one off.

In the mid 1980s our business started to slow down and this included the loss of the Hawaii contract. There were layoffs and a reshuffling of crews. The people who were laid off went on to other jobs, mostly in the towboat industry. For those who remained the wages stayed about the same, but the crews on the *Edith* and *Duwamish* were on call which made life uncertain. Knowing that after the year was up we would be back to two weeks on and two off made it easier to cope with. Each crew worked 12 months on the *Anne Carlander* with two crews working two weeks on and two weeks off. Then they shifted to the *Edith Lovejoy* with one crew and were on call working 15 days a month for 6 months. Following that the crew moved to the *Duwamish* for 6 months, again working 15 days a month. When the crew had completed the time on the *Duwamish* the rotation began all over again. While this rotation sounds complicated it was fair for everyone. During this time the *Pachena* was laid up and put up for sale. After she was sold the new owner from Alaska renamed her *Lumberman*. She is still being used today.

Tugboat Life (1970 to 1998)
Chapter 35
Tug *Duwamish*: Port Alberni and Gold River Trips
Fire on *Duwamish*

When our crew rotated to the *Duwamish* in the mid 1980s it was a learning experience for me. I had run only single screw boats and the *Duwamish* was twin screw. She was 100.4 feet long, 29 feet wide and 13.5 feet draft with two V16-149 GMC diesel engines for a total of 2200 hp. The former owner, Inland Marine, had her built in Orange County, Texas, in 1976.

Most of the trips on the Duwamish were to Port Alberni. We made three five-day Alberni trips per month. Later we started hauling out of Gold River, BC, (another port farther north) on the west coast of Vancouver Island. Gold River lies 110 miles north of Cape Flattery and is similar to Port Alberni in that it is 25 miles inland through a narrow channel. The approach to the inlet is across a shallow bay called Nootka Sound.

When approaching Nootka Sound on our way to Gold River the water shallows up to about 15 fathoms. Incoming ocean swells, predominately southwest, start to increase in size as they hit this shallow water. The entrance narrows to 2 miles then opens to a small inland bay with a cluster of islands. Further in is a narrower channel that leads to Gold River. At the end of this channel is our destination, the Gold River Pulp and Paper Mill. The town of Gold River lies several miles inland from the mill. These scenic inlets on the west side of Vancouver Island are all similar in that they are narrow with heavily wooded hills rising steeply from the water's edge.

Tug *Duwamish* and barge *Cape Flattery*

The trips to Port Alberni on the *Duwamish* were becoming routine until August 7, 1988. We had left Port Alberni in the evening towing the *Cape Flattery* loaded with newsprint for Seattle. I had gone off shift at midnight and Don Seabury had taken over just before departing the Alberni inlet. At 1:10 am I heard an engine slow down so I started to get out of bed when the door to my room opened and Dick Harmon said, "Get up! We're on fire!" I quickly got dressed and headed for the wheelhouse. The area outside my room and in the wheelhouse was filled with a thick haze of smoke. Don Seabury, the mate, said, "We have a fire in the engine room," and left to help below decks. I grabbed the radio and informed Tofino Vessel Traffic of our situation. Wayne Johnson, the engineer, hollered up through the stairwell that he was going to activate the CO^2 fire system and asked me to shut down the engines from the wheelhouse. I pushed the shutdown switches and nothing happened. Apparently the port engine was already dead from the fire. The starboard shutdown switch had apparently also been killed by the flames. I then heard the CO^2 activate. The starboard main engine and auxiliary engines died and the lights went out. This had all happened in about 5 or 10 minutes.

Next, someone yelled, "Watch out! Here comes the barge!" I looked out the wheelhouse door and saw an eerie red glow through the smoke. The barge slid by us, missing the tug by one foot. By now the smoke was so thick I couldn't see the barge except for the running light. The barge continued on until it came to the end of the tow wire. The wire came tight and the barge stopped. The tow wire slacked down and anchored us to the bottom.

We still had one VHF radio working off battery power and were in touch with Tofino Vessel Traffic. They alerted emergency services and any vessels in our vicinity. They also called our night dispatcher and passed on our situation. In the meantime Dave Grant and Dick Harmon were gathering our emergency gear, portable radio, survival suits and flashlights, and moving them up to the bow away from the fire. We also put our life raft cannister over the side in case the fire erupted on the deck.

After about 30 minutes we noticed that a mooring line stowed flat on the deck on the port side alongside the stack was starting to smoke. The bulkhead outside the "fidley" (an area inside the outer door above the engine room with a grated floor) was hot to the touch. We could see a red glow through the blackened porthole and knew the fire had rekindled.

One of the crew members said, "Let's get off this thing." I didn't think there was any danger of an explosion so I said we needed to stay onboard and do what we could to save the boat.

By this time a tug and a fishing vessel arrived on the scene and were standing by. We were informed that a fast response Canadian Coast Guard vessel was under way from Bamfield and would arrive in about 30 minutes with a pump. The only option we had at that time was to start dumping 5 gallon buckets of seawater into the air vent above the engine room. After dumping the first bucket there was a huge eruption of black smoke from the vent so we thought it was helping.

By the time the fast response vessel arrived at 0315 AM the fire seemed to be dying down. We retrieved their pump and ran a fire hose from it into the vent with the nozzle set to fog and pumped saltwater into the engine room for about 15 minutes. Two Canadian Coast Guardsmen had arrived with the fast response vessel and they advised us to shut down the pump, let things cool down, and wait for awhile to see what happened.

At 0430 our engineer and one of the Canadian Coast Guard men entered the engine room with a fire hose and declared the fire out. We closed the door and waited another hour before going back in to check the damage. When we reentered at 0530 one wood cabinet in the fidley was still burning. One of the crew members picked up a can of Pepsi that was lying on the floor and shook it up squirting out the fire!

We found the damage to be extensive especially around the port engine and the overhead above it. The air was extremely foul, smelling of burnt rubber and plastic. It was a strange sight: areas of heavy damage and yet a few feet away areas left untouched. At the front of the engine room a see-through tube on the day tank (close to the source of the fire) escaped undamaged. If the fire had melted that tube it would have introduced 1000 gallons of diesel fuel into the fire with a much different outcome.

Tugboat Life (1970 to 1998)
Chapter 36
After the Fire

By 0500 the situation was getting under control. The Canadian National Fisheries Vessel *Tanu* was on the scene. The other vessels that had been standing by were released by the Coast Guard and had gone on their way. At 0900 a small tug from Port Alberni arrived to tow us to Seattle. By late afternoon we were in the Strait of Juan de Fuca when the *Pachena* arrived. They had been sent to our rescue by the Seattle office and took over the tow from the Canadian tug. With power from the *Pachena* we started up the tow winch engine and pulled in some wire to shorten our total length, which included two tugs and one barge. The *Pachena* hooked a tow line to our bow and off we headed for Seattle.

We were riding a dead ship. It was quiet without the engines running and we heard lots of sounds we wouldn't hear over normal engine noise. The water and air bubbles washed by the outside of the hull and occasionally some object bumped the outside. We heard creaking and groaning sounds. With no power to cook food we had to rely on cold sandwiches and dry cereal in the morning. With no need to navigate or steer, our only task was a radio watch and occasionally checking for leaks. These gave us time to rest and reflect on what we had experienced.

The *Pachena* had us tied up at Pier 7 in Seattle early the next morning. At 0800 management arrived and Wayne Johnson and I were asked to write a minute by minute account of the fire. We had already written these accounts on our way into Seattle; they were impressed when we immediately handed them over.

We had all inhaled smoke during the fire but Wayne had got the worst of it. He had tried to enter the engine room at the beginning of the fire and had received a heavy dose of smoke. Dave Grant had injured his knee while fighting the fire so we were all sent to the hospital for a check up. Wayne came down with cancer a few years later. It could have been caused by his smoke inhalation, so with his doctor's advice he quit tug boating. He entered the educational field as a high school English teacher.

The official cause of the fire was a transformer in the middle of the engine room that had failed and burst into flame. Art Olsen the company's chief engineer stated his suspicion that the fire had more likely started from a coffee can holding paint brushes and cleaning solvent that he noticed stored on the grated floor in the fidley above the port engine. As the boat rolled in the ocean swell that can may have tipped over and spilled flammable solvent onto the hot engine.

Our crew was asked to submit suggestions from what we had learned to make the boat safer and prevent a fire from happening again. Wayne compiled a list of suggestions from the crew and produced an extensive letter for management. I followed up with a letter with the suggestion that a video monitoring system be installed in the engine room on our tugs. When the *Duwamish* was rebuilt most of the suggestions were incorporated into the rebuild. The video monitoring system was rejected because an improved alarm system had been installed and it was felt the video monitor could cause a distraction in the wheelhouse at night. Improvements included were a portable fire pump in a locker on the boat deck, covers for engine room blower vents, emergency lighting system and escape hatch and ladder at the forward end of the engine room. All the tugs in the fleet moved their survival suits from each stateroom to storage in their wheelhouses. This would be the most likely gathering place in an emergency.

The *Duwamish* continued working for Puget Sound Freight Lines until 1998 when it was sold to Brusco Towing Company. On December 30, 2002, she sank off Florence, Oregon, in a storm with 30 foot seas. The US Coast Guard rescued three from a life raft and another man in the water. One man was missing and never found. She had left Aberdeen with a loaded log barge for California. The barge did not sink and was retrieved by another tug. I had experienced those conditions with that tug twice on the coast and it had handled them well. It makes me wonder what had happened?

Tugboat Life 37 (1970 to 1998)
Chapter 37
Close Calls

During my 28 years with Puget Sound Freight Lines hauling freight, there were a few accidents and close calls. The company had one crew member fatality during those years. A man fell overboard and drowned when he came to work late at night with no other crew members around. That was the only on the job death during my 28 years.

One time when we were landing a barge at Pier 7 in Seattle, Wayne Johnson the engineer, stepped off the barge onto the dock with the end of a mooring line and placed it on a cleat. Don Seabury, the mate, was on the barge with a radio controlling the landing and I was on the tug. As the barge slid into the correct mooring position the mate instructed a deckhand to tie the line down while the heavily loaded barge was still moving. The line came snapping tight and broke at the barge end. The line snapped like a broken rubber band and flew back onto the dock hitting Wayne in the chest. He was wearing a life jacket but it still knocked the wind out of him and broke a couple of ribs.

On a trip to Powell River, B.C., we were hooking up to a barge that another tug had left there. Normally the heavy anchor chain type bridles (chains in a V shape leading from both front corners of the barge to a center point and attached to a single strand of chain that the tow wire hooks to) was hanging on the bow of the barge with two rope lines. One line was holding up the bridles and one was for hauling the end aboard and hooking up to the tow wire. The mate handed down the end of the retrieval line to the men on the deck of the tug. Then he untied that line from the cleat. Nobody noticed that there was only one line. On the tug, the single line was wrapped around the capstan. A capstan is a heavy metal cylinder flared at each end and attached to a shaft that turns; the friction of the several wraps around it starts pulling in the line. The mate started to untie the line from the cleat and the weight of the bridles suddenly took over and pulled the line at a high rate of speed backwards. The line at the capstan was pulled out of the hands of the man who held it and it whipped around the capstan. The end of the line whacked the deckhand two or three times at a high rate of speed before he could move. It was like being hit by a 2x4. I was on the deck above him running the capstan controller and he was out of my sight. I was mesmerized by the sight of his glove flying up in the air doing slow loops, like in a horror movie when the monster chops off the victim's hand. The force of the blows knocked him to the deck and gave him some bad bruises but didn't break any bones.

Another accident occurred at a Seattle dock. We were tying the tug up at Pier 42 in Seattle and the mate was tending the bowline. I leaned out the wheelhouse window and said, "Give me a little more slack," so I could back-up further. He took most of the wraps off the cleat so it would pull out the slack I needed. As it came tight the line momentarily hung up then snapped loose. I looked out of the window and said, "Are you ok?" He said nonchalantly, "I broke my arm." My reply was, "You're kidding?" But it was true. The force of the line jerking out of his hand had broken his arm bone just above the wrist. We all learned that day that you don't grip a line that you are feeding through a cleat, you hold on to it with the tips of your fingers.

At another time, two of our crew members, Dick Harmon and Dave Grant, were working unloading newsprint inside a barge at a dock in Seattle. The barge had a rough trip on its way into Seattle and some of the load had shifted. The two men were on forklifts side-by-side trying to lift newsprint rolls off the top of the pile. The rolls were stuck. Dick stepped off his forklift to see what was hanging up. Just as he stepped free of the protection of the forklift cab the pile of 2000 lb rolls collapsed on top of him. He dropped to the floor in the fetal position as rolls slammed down around him then more rolls on top of those. Miraculously they had all missed him but he badly bruised his knees when he dropped to the floor and had to go to the emergency room and then home to recuperate.

I think Ken Miller, a mate, wins the prize for the most close calls. He fell off barges into the water two or three times. He was feeling sick on a trip to Port Angeles one night and went to the hospital when he arrived. They found that a large blood vessel in the upper part of his leg had broken. The doctor said he wouldn't have lasted much longer. On another trip to Port Alberni after arriving from Seattle, he asked the customs broker to give him a ride to the doctor because he had not been feeling well that night on shift. The doctor found that he had suffered a heart attack. After all that, he is still kicking and doing well in retirement.

I have always tried to be aware of possible dangers, but my own worst accident occurred because I did not see the danger. I was driving a forklift at Pier 7 in Seattle unloading newsprint into a warehouse. The warehouse had high ceilings that were supported by large metal posts. I set down my load and backed away. Then I swung around to head for the door. One of the posts was lined up and obscured by the mast on the forklift (a blind spot) and I slammed into it at about 5 miles an hour. The sudden stop catapulted me into the windshield and a sharp part of the windshield wiper motor raked across the top of my head. Blood ran down my forehead. After I had regained my senses I drove back out to the barge and asked the mate to check the damage. He took one look and said, "We're going to the emergency room." At the hospital they cleaned up the two inch wound and added about 12 stitches. They told me not to go to sleep for 12 hours in case of concussion. We went back to work and finished the rest of our two week shift.

I had a couple of other close calls over the years. One time a pile of pallet boards fell and missed me by inches. Another time a line broke on the back deck of the tug and threw a 20 lb shackle at me. It hit the back of the wheelhouse a few feet from where I was standing, leaving a large dent in the steel wall. I never saw it go by but looking at its line of travel I don't know how it missed me. Maybe there are guardian angels?

Tugboat Life (1970 to 1998)
Chapter 38
First Trip to California

In the mid 1980s while I was crewed on the tug *Duwamish* I got word that we would be hauling a load of newsprint from Crofton, B.C, to Long Beach, California. I had made a few trips down to the Columbia River but this would be my first trip to California. This was going to be interesting. I was pleased to have a mate that had several years of experience in ocean towing.

Crofton is on the east side of Vancouver Island about 30 miles north of Victoria, B.C., Longshoremen and mill workers did the loading and the tug crew did the final securing of the load with cargo straps and large inflatable air bags to fill any gaps between the rolls. The barge was the *Cape Flattery* it had an asphalt deck so 2x8 lumbers, spaced a few inches apart, were used to create airspace between the rolls and the deck.

For our trip down the coast we navigated with Loran and following the 125th longitude line down to Cape Mendocino on the California coast. This straight-line course would take us 25 to 30 miles off the coast in the area of the Columbia River then back in to 10 to 12 miles at Cape Mendocino. Then we changed course for Point Arguello south of San Francisco. Another course change led us through Santa Barbara Channel. A final course change took us to the entrance to Long Beach where we picked up a harbor pilot.

Loran is an electronic receiver that collects signals from land-based transmitters and calculates the ship's position. Then it displays the position in the form of two large numbers. These two numbers refer to a Loran chart that has intersecting numbered lines and where the two lines cross is the ship's position.

The mate produced a position report each morning before going off shift at 0600, which I used in my morning report to our office in Seattle. The report included our position, speed and distance traveled for the last 24 hours, weather and sea conditions, and ETA at destination.

We got underway at about midday after two days, loading 3200 tons at Crofton. By late afternoon we had added one shot of surge gear (90 feet of heavy anchor chain) between the end of the tow wire and the barge bridles. The "surge gear" helps soften the shock to the tow wire, from the ocean swell. We were in the outer Strait of Juan de Fuca and as the sun was setting the weather was turning bad. The sky was black with thunder clouds and wind was starting to blow. Normally I headed for a safe place to hide from this kind of weather but I had been told many times that this tug and barge could handle it, so we kept on going. By morning we were midway down the Washington coast. The wind was 30 to 40 knots and the swell was 30 feet and we were running with just enough speed to maintain our course. By the next morning we had gone backwards 4 or 5 miles but the storm was moving on and we were starting to move forward again.

The rest of the trip down the coast was fairly nice except for a short stretch off San Francisco where the weather kicked up again for 5 or 6 hours. On the morning of the fifth day, as I was going on shift, we were entering the Santa Barbara Channel. I thought I had died and gone to heaven. The sky was clear, the wind was calm, and the sea was alive with wildlife. There were all kinds of sea birds including pelicans, seagulls and more. There was also dolphins, whales, and sharks everywhere! I had both side doors in the wheelhouse open and I was so busy looking at wildlife I hardly had time to navigate.

We tied up at Pier 2 at Long Beach and after opening the barge doors we found that the rolls at the aft door had shifted and were leaning into the door. The barge *Cape Flattery* has two cargo doors and the aft door had been loaded differently than the front door. The lumber on the floor had been laid down front to back and in the rest of the load the lumber had been side to side. This allowed the load to shift during the storm and it caused damage to several rolls. The unloading took two days and I had a chance to visit with some long time friends who lived in the area. The trip back was uneventful except for a minor engine problem. We stopped and shut down and drifted for about thirty minutes ten miles off the mouth of the Columbia River while the engineer and mate corrected the problem. It was at night and the ocean was "flat as a pancake." I don't think I have ever seen it that calm! We arrived back in Seattle after being gone 14 days.

Newsprint rolls: Before & After a Storm

Duwamish and barge *Cape Flattery* (California Coast)

Tugboat Life (1970 to 1998)
Chapter 39
Second trip to California

We made a second trip to Long Beach, California, a short time later in January. On this trip we loaded at Elk Falls near Campbell River, British Columbia. When we left Seattle it was snowing, and a few inches of snow had built up on the barge roof. When we arrived at Elk Falls it was raining and the snow on the barge was melting. With all that water running around it was inevitable that some would get inside of the barge. This would come back to haunt us later on.

After getting underway with our load, we ran into the same kind of weather on the Washington coast as we had on the trip before, high winds and 30 foot seas. After a period of time the wind switched from southeast to northwest and was on our tail.

The ride became much nicer but the farther south we went the larger the swell got and we had to slow down to lessen the strain on the tow wire. Here my lack of ocean towing experience came into play. Where the tow wire wraps onto the drum it exerts a tremendous amount of pressure on the wire beneath it. I was reluctant to let out more wire for fear of losing it all overboard. On the trip before, the mate (Bill) who was experienced with ocean towing, had taken care of what is called "refreshing the tow wire" on a daily basis. He did this by starting up the tow winch engine and powering out some wire with the brake on to decrease the wear in any one place.

I was always off shift during this process and didn't have a clue how he handled it. Harvey (the mate) and Wayne (the engineer) with me on this trip had the same level of experience I had. We had daily discussions as to whether any damage was being caused by the extreme pressure on the tow wire and winch from the large following swell off the southern California Coast. We later learned that it was, and some of the wire below the point where the wire wrapped onto the drum was crushed and the whole tow wire had to be replaced after this trip to the tune of about $10,000.00.

But this wasn't all the damage. On arrival at Long Beach when the barge was unloaded we found water damage to several of the rolls of newsprint. We had tried to guard against that by setting the rolls at the stern on pallet boards, to raise them off the deck (where any water in the barge would gather), but the water had splashed up the wall in the rough weather.

On our trip back north we headed for Gold River on the west coast of Vancouver Island to take on a load of wood pulp for Seattle. The trip up the coast turned out to be rough with two days of bad weather.

On both of these California trips we had good crews that got along well. On the second trip the deckhand and the engineer who were on opposite shifts started playing practical jokes on each other. One time the deckhand went down to the engine room where the engineer had a plastic bucket turned up-side down that he sat on. The bottom of the bucket had a lip around the outside of about one half inch. He filled it with water and covered it with a rag. When the engineer came on shift and sat on the bucket, he got a wet bottom.

The dock at Gold River is at the mouth of a large salmon spawning river. After we were tied up there were several large spawned out king salmon swimming around the boat. The engineer managed to catch one in a dip net. He put the half dead salmon in the shower stall just before the deckhand was going to take a shower. When the deckhand stepped into the shower the salmon came alive and started leaping around, It scared the hell out of him. We all got a good laugh on his behalf.

That reminds me of a prank played on me by Darren Marsh. I was driving a forklift while unloading a barge at Pier 7 in Seattle. I was driving on the dock and delivering newsprint rolls from the barge into the warehouse. While negotiating a dark aisle between rows of newsprint in the warehouse, Darren managed to climb onto the roof of my forklift and as I was setting down my load he stuck his head over the edge of the roof right in front of my face. At that time in the 1970s he had shoulder length hair and with his hair hanging down in that dark space my first thought was a huge spider. It scared the heck out of me.

Arriving back in Seattle after our second trip to California and unloading our barge we all went home. We'd been gone 29 days. I said to Harvey the mate,

"That wasn't that bad. Are you going on the next trip?" He said, "NO WAY! That was terrible!"

Tugboat Life (1970 to 1998)
Chapter 40
Start Tandem Towing

For the first ten years at Puget Sound Freight Lines we were towing just one barge. This made us the envy of some of the Canadian tugboaters who were usually towing two and sometimes three barges at one time.

This easy-going life didn't last forever. We were crewed on the *Anne Carlander* and loading a barge in Port Angles when I got a call from our office in Seattle. They wanted to know what equipment I would need to tow two barges. This sounded interesting so I asked them if this was a long-term arrangement or a temporary thing. They said for now it would be temporary. I ordered two 100 foot soft lines with 6 foot cables with eyes on each end. These would be used to couple the two barges together for towing around Puget Sound and out to Port Angeles. With 100 feet of line it would allow them to bounce around in a heavy swell. This worked, but the 100 foot lines were awkward to handle on the narrow deck on the outer edge of the barges.

When it turned out to be more than a one-time thing, Captain Don Nystrom suggested we use an item called a Canadian link. The link was a heavy piece of metal with a hole in the middle and flexible sockets on each end. The tow wires were cut 550 feet from the end and the resulting two ends were inserted into the sockets of the Canadian link. The wire ends are flared out in the socket and melted zinc was poured into the socket. This secures the wire in the socket. Links were installed on the *Edith Lovejoy* and the *Anne Carlander*. The tow winches were the same on both these vessels. The "fairleads" (the rollers that thread the wire evenly on to the drum of the winch, like a fishing reel) were offset which allowed the large link to thread through onto the drum when not in use. Through trial and error we soon refined the most efficient and safe way for departures and arrivals with two barges.

Second barge hooked up

Hooking up wire bridles for second barge

When towing two barges in tandem, the second barge is out of sight behind the first one, because of the 20 foot high deck houses unless you turn a corner. One of the crews on the *Edith Lovejoy* was towing two barges from Seattle to Port Angeles when they ran into rough weather in the area of Port Townsend. It was dark and nasty with west wind of 30 or 40 knots, creating a 6 to 8 foot choppy swell. After two or three hours they had worked their way out to the area of New Dungeness. When they heard a call from a ship to the Vessel Traffic System, the caller had just passed a barge adrift on its own! The captain on the tug immediately turned to see if he had two barges and by golly - one was missing! He called the night dispatcher who decided to call another tug company at Port Townsend to retrieve their barge. After they had tied up the first barge at Port Angeles, they had to run back to Port Townsend for their lost barge.

Pier 7 in Seattle had become our home port. It included three large warehouses with office space above one of them. Pier 7 is a short way up the Duwamish River, which is also called the West Waterway. When departing Pier 7 with two barges, we tied them side by side. Then we hooked up to one of them with the tow wire. This is the way we towed the two barges out of the waterway and into deep water in the harbor. Next, we let out the tow wire until the Canadian Link was in the middle of the back deck of the tug. A crew member on the second barge handed down the retrieval line, the towing pendant was retrieved and hooked up to the Canadian link. The crew member on the barge untied the lines that held the two barges together, and then came back aboard the tug. Next I dropped out some more tow wire and slowly stretched the barges out, one in front of the other. Then we were underway.

There was one occasion when one of the tug crews was doing one of these hook-ups in Seattle harbor with the wind blowing 25 to 30 knots. Through miscommunications the barges got cut apart too early and one took off downwind. The tug with the other barge in tow took off in hot pursuit. They managed to recapture it a few hundred yards before it smashed into the Edgewater Hotel that extends out over the water on the Seattle waterfront. For most of our arrivals at other ports we used "assist" tugs to take one barge from us and either land it or hang on to it until we had landed the other one.

At Port Townsend and Port Angeles we usually landed our barges without the help of an assist tug.

Upon arrival we shortened up the tow wire, cut loose from the first barge and brought it alongside the tug. Then we let the second barge hang on the tow wire. As we approached the dock I let the tow wire pay out and lie on the bottom which anchored that second barge while still on the tow wire. After landing the first barge we pulled in the wire and landed the second barge.

Towing two barges with the *Pachena* was a little more complicated. An under rider drum with 500 ft of wire with eyes on each end was mounted on the back deck with an air powered motor. It's the same idea as the Canadian link except the "under rider" wire has to be dealt with on a separate drum and is hooked up at the same junction as the first barge.

The *Duwamish* was the easiest tug for handling two barges because it had two tow wires. We just had to be careful, that while letting out the tow wires, we got the correct distance between the barges.

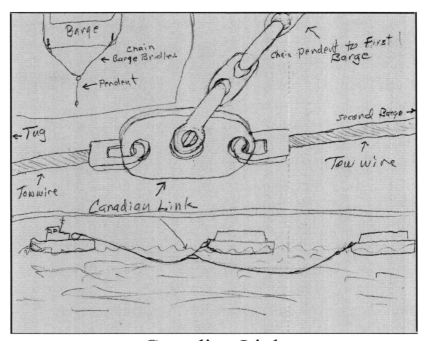

Canadian Link

Tugboat Life (1970 to 1998)
Chapter 41
Interesting Things on the Water

I've seen some interesting things out on the water over the years. One late night coming out of Bellingham with one barge in tow the water was glowing. Every wavelet as far as I could see was glowing as if it had a light bulb in it. The tow wire underwater all the way to the barge was glowing white. The barge looked like it was riding on a carpet of light. Any fish that was moving in the water was like a light bulb on the move. During transits through Saratoga Passage between Whidbey Island and Camano Island in the 1960s the tug had a white halo around it at night as huge schools of hake were moving away from the boat. Back then we thought it was phosphorus in the water but we've learned since then it's billions of tiny organisms that produce a flash of light when disturbed.

Gary Campbell, one of the Captains at Puget Sound Freight Lines, told me he had seen several elephant sea over the years. I had never seen one and was beginning to wonder if Gary knew what he was talking about? We were crewed together on the *Anne Carlander* and northbound in the area of Edmonds, Washington. I was in the galley when Gary yelled for me to come to the wheelhouse. He handed me the binoculars and pointed at a black object about a quarter-mile ahead. There it was: a large male elephant sea distinguishable by its large nose. Only older males venture this far north. I would see two more of these spectacular animals in the next few years. I saw one at Turn Point at the north end of the San Juan Islands. As I approached him he went from vertical to horizontal on the surface of the water. He was breathing hard and I saw the steam coming from his mouth. He was loading up on oxygen, preparing to dive. They feed in very deep water and can stay down for a long time. I passed within 50 feet of him and got a good look. He was huge maybe 12 to 15 feet long with a foot-long floppy trunk like nose.

I've seen the northern lights on several occasions while traveling the waters of Puget Sound and Southern British Columbia. This far south they are usually displayed in white but there have been a couple of times they were in "Technicolor". One special night in the Strait of Georgia I watched a display in an array of vivid colors as they danced across the sky.

On a trip to Port Alberni on the tug *Duwamish* we were near Port Townsend. I was just going off shift at midnight and Darrel McCormick was coming on watch. I had left the wheelhouse and entered my stateroom when Darrel yelled, "Come back to the wheelhouse quick." When I reached the wheelhouse he pointed to an object streaking across the western sky. It was traveling from left to right and leaving a white smoke trail behind it. The object was up in the sky higher than an airplane would fly and following the contour of the earth. Later we learned that a Russian satellite had entered the atmosphere and burned up.

On another occasion I saw a large meteorite enter the atmosphere at night; explode into two pieces and burn.

One day I was in the wheelhouse of the *Anne Carlander* parked at the Rayonier Dock at Port Angeles opposite the east end of Ediz Hook. I noticed two jet planes approaching from the east and looking like they intended to land. Ediz Hook has a short runway for helicopters and I knew it was much too short for a jet to land on. When the two jets, side by side, reached the runway they stopped in mid-air about 200 feet above the ground in front of the approach tower. My mouth dropped open, "What the heck!" They each rotated 360 degrees one way, then the other way, and blasted off into regular flight. Then I realized there is a jet called a Harrier that can do that. I had never seen one before.

Another interesting event was told to me by an older, distinguished gentleman who had many years at sea and was working with me as mate on the tug Anne Carlander. He told me a story of a strange encounter he had at sea many years before. He was ferrying a fishing vessel from Alaska to Seattle at the end of the fishing season in the 1950s. They were crossing the Gulf of Alaska where the weather was fairly rough and it was the middle of the night.

Alone in the wheelhouse he noticed a blip on the radar and figured it was another ship closing on his position. As it got closer he could see one small square green light. When it got even closer he suddenly realized this object was not on the water but above the water! As it got closer he called for the rest of the crew to come take a look. It was shaped like a cigar, maybe 300 feet long and 50 feet above the water. He was leaning out an open window and had a flashlight in his hand. He turned the flashlight on and pointed it at the object. It immediately turned 90 degrees and shot away. They watched it on the radar and estimated it was traveling 600 MPH.

Sea lions perched on our mooring buoy in Tacoma, Washington. We had to approach and almost bump the buoy before these guys would move so we could tie up our barge.

Tugboat Life (1970 to 1998)
Chapter 42
Boat Maintenance and Failures

The crews and homebase engineers kept the tugs and barges we used at Puget Sound Freight Lines in excellent condition. We had a port engineer and two full time shore-side engineers. The deckhands onboard kept track of the engine room and kept it spotlessly clean and took care of some light maintenance, like oil changes. When we arrived at Pier 7 in Seattle the shore side engineers always came aboard and checked the engine room for any major repairs.

In the late 1970s the company was offered new Caterpillar main engines by the Caterpillar Company for the same cost as an engine rebuild, about $100,000. These were 1100 hp D399, 16 cylinder new engines that normally cost probably twice that price. Puget Sound Freight Lines bought two and put one in the *Edith Lovejoy* and saved the other one for future use.

When it came time for one of the engines on the *Edith Lovejoy* or the *Anne Carlander* to be rebuilt the shore side engineering crew and a couple of other helpers pulled out the engine and replaced it with the engine waiting in reserve. They got this down to about a five day process and it happened about once every year or two with one boat or the other. The engine taken out was rebuilt by the shore side engineers and would be ready for the next exchange. These engines were not small like a car engine; they were the size of a car, about 12 feet long 7 feet tall and 5 feet wide. Sections of the engine room ceiling, containing two engine room blowers, were removed to make access possible. A large crane was brought in to do the lifting.

Because of the excellent maintenance program we had very few mechanical failures. One I can remember was while northbound in Haro Strait on the west side of San Juan Island. The reverse gear on the *Anne Carlander* decided to quit. It was in the morning and the weather was calm. We called for help and another of our company tugs was sent out to retrieve us.

A more dangerous failure occurred when departing Crofton, B.C., on the tug *Duwamish* with two loaded barges in tow. The steering suddenly went hard over to the right and stayed there. We were in a narrow channel at the northeast end of Saltspring Island between Saltspring and Wallace Island. We were surrounded by rocky beaches and underwater reefs. There were no soft landing spots there. I used the engines to try to keep going in a straight line by running the port engine in reverse to pull the bow to the left and the starboard at full RPM. The smoke was pouring out of the stack and I was slowly losing the battle. Luckily I had three engineers on board who knew the systems; one was on as mate, one as deckhand, and one as the engineer. They tore into the problem like a mad bull after a matador. Parts were flying as they dug through cupboards trying to find replacement parts for the steering system. As I was about to give up and make a desperate effort to turn a circle where there was not enough room to turn they found the right circuit board and popped it in. The steering came back to life. It was like winning the world series of engine repair!

Then there were the self produced problems. I caught the tow wire in the propeller three times at Puget Sound Freight Lines over the 28 year period. One of those times I managed to get it out myself by shifting into reverse momentarily and it spit the wire out with no damage. I wasn't always that lucky.

One time when we were in Port Angeles harbor, maneuvering close to a barge, the tow-wire pendant we were using at that time became lodged between the propeller and the Kort nozzle. We drifted against a log-tow storage and tied up. We had to call for a diver to come and cut it out with an underwater cutting torch. This "foul-up" cost us 6 hours of time and the price of a diver and new tow pendant.

On another occasion we were hooking up a tandem tow at Powell River, B.C. when the tow pendant from one of the barges got sucked into the propeller. I managed to get the engine out of gear just as I saw it happen. I called a nearby harbor tug for help. We had him hook on to our bow and pull gently. As I saw the tow wire start to take a strain I quickly went in and out of reverse; the wire jumped free! The captain on the assist tug couldn't believe my good luck. I called it "good experience."

PART – III
Tugboat Life (1998 to 2006)
Chapter 43
Olympic Tug and Barge
A New Employer and New Experiences

In April of 1998 we got a big surprise that nobody wanted. It came as a letter informing all employees that Puget Sound Freight Lines, Marine Division, was going out of business in two weeks. This would affect every person including the president and vice president and all their staff, the engineering department, the warehouse management and crews, and all the tugboat crews.

The only survivors were the vice president, who retired with a pension, and the head of the engineering department, who stayed on to manage the buildings and equipment.

The tug crews consisted of 16 people at that time; 12 would be gone immediately. I and three others stayed on an extra month to empty out the warehouses and tie up the tugs and barges. We delivered the cargo from the warehouses back to the original shippers. On the last day we tied up the remaining 2 tugs and 4 barges. We packed off our personal gear for the last time, locked the doors, and went to lunch with the management and office crews.

The lumber industry was in a bad slump. We were considered to be part of that business. Because of that slow down all people who lost their jobs could get scholarships for re-education. Three of the laid-off crewmembers took advantage of that help. All the others soon found other work in the towing business.

I had sent out résumés to several companies and had an interview at Olympic Tug and Barge in Seattle, I had been told to call them when I was through working. We were through on a Thursday so Friday morning I called them. I was told to come to their office on Monday morning for another interview. I was offered a job as a mate and went to work a few days later. I had worked the previous 28 years as a captain so this would be a new experience. I told myself all I had to do was a good job and things would be okay. What I didn't know and would find out in about two months was that I had actually been hired as captain on a specific job coming up in July. In the first week of June the captain I was working with moved to a management job in the office and I took over as captain. In the meantime I was working on the tug *Catherine Quigg* as a mate.

We were a three man crew on the *Catherine Quigg*, captain, mate and a deckhand-engineer. Our main job was being attached to a barge "bunkering" ships in Tacoma and Seattle harbors with an occasional trip to one of the refineries. Bunkering is fueling ships with a petroleum product called bunker oil. Bunker oil is produced at a refinery from the distillation (heating) of crude oil. When the crude oil is heated it separates into different products such as propane gas, naphtha, gasoline, jet fuel, lubricating oil, and diesel oils. Finally all that is left is bunker fuel and a residue that is used for road blacktopping.

Olympic was providing only "bunker oil" which is commonly known as "black oil". The other types of fuel are called "clean oil". To haul clean oil in a barge that had been hauling black oil it would first have to be thoroughly cleaned with high pressure steam. To handle black oil, the oil has to be heated to 150 degrees to get it into a liquid form. If it cools below 90 degrees it starts to get too hard to pump and the cooler it gets the thicker it gets until it has the consistency of tar. The oil in the barge starts to cool at a rate of about 2 degrees per hour so there is a time period of about 36 hours to get the product delivered. The barge tanks are equipped with a series of pipes that hot steam can be pumped through to reheat the oil if ever needed. Shipyards can supply the steam; I can remember that happening only once in my 8 years working for Olympic Tug and Barge

Oil is measured by its viscosity (its thickness) and black oil is 1500 to 2000 viscosity. When a ship orders fuel it specifies a certain viscosity and most ships use 380 viscosity. To get to that number the distributor has to blend the black oil with a product called cutter. Cutter is a type of dirty diesel oil. The orders are in tons and it takes 6.45 barrels to equal one ton. One oil barrel is 42 gallons.

A refinery produces the black oil from crude oil and Olympic Tug and Barge hauls it in large tanks in barge hulls to a distributor. There are several around

Puget Sound. The distributor receives an order from a shipping company to fuel one of its ships then Olympic transports the product to alongside the ship in one of its barges and pumps it aboard using a long black hose of 6 to 8 inches in diameter.

When I went to work for Olympic Tug and Barge they had 5 barges and 4 tugs. Three of the barges had 25,000 barrel capacity. One had 45,000 barrel capacity and another had 90,000 barrel capacity. My crew was using one of the smaller barges. The loading and unloading was handled by a shore-based tanker-man who would meet us at the job site. Olympic had several shore-based tanker-men who were dispatched to each fueling and the tug crews coordinated directly with them the time they needed to arrive.

Alyssa Ann with barge Norton

This barge, *Norton*, was equipped to do its own oil fuel blending. It carried bunker fuel and cutter and a system to do the blending as it delivered the fuel to a ship. It also had a heating system to keep the fuel hot. It ran heated peanut oil through pipes inside the oil tanks.

It was a challenge meeting the exact fuel requirements of ships from all over the world.
A loaded oil barge, approaching and preparing to tie alongside a ship for a fuel transfer.

The *Norton* fully loaded is approaching a ship. It is going very slowly at this point of the approach. The 45,000 barrel (1,890,000 gallons) load is extremely heavy and hard to stop.

Tugboat Life (1998 to 2006)
Chapter 44
Olympic Tug and Barge: Rough Trip in Rosario Strait

The management style at Olympic Tug and Barge was different from what I had been used to at Dunlap Towing and Puget Sound Freight Lines. Olympic was an oil transportation company and had to work with many layers of regulations, both company policy and government. This created a different work atmosphere. This would lead to some problems for me down the road but for the present I was just glad to have found a new job and was busy learning all about it.

Mike, the first captain I started working with at Olympic, was a rather high strung type of guy. I had a few problems getting along with him first as captain and later as the port captain. The first time I noticed something wrong was when we were entering Seattle harbor at night with a barge alongside. I was in bed when the deckhand called me to get up to help with the landing. As I entered the wheelhouse with Mike running the boat from up on the flying bridge, I noticed a crab buoy dead ahead. I stuck my head out the side door and yelled to him over the noise of the engines, "There's a buoy dead ahead." Mike came scrambling down from above and started yelling at me. He hollered, "You don't need to yell at me about something that is completely obvious." Of course I was just making sure we didn't end up with a buoy line in the propeller. This upset me some. I hastily grabbed my equipment to head up on the barge for the landing and accidentally hit the button on a portable horn which blasted loud in the wheelhouse. Mike began yelling louder at me to, "Get the hell out of his wheelhouse." I stomped up onto the barge with steam coming out of my ears and told the deckhand I needed to get away from Mike before things escalated beyond words. After we had arrived at our dock and I went back to the boat Mike apologized for yelling. My thought was, if you need to apologize you shouldn't have yelled in the first place.

Life at Olympic settled into a routine of moving barges and fueling ships around Tacoma and Seattle harbor with a week on and a week off. We all carried pagers and usually had a schedule of up coming jobs, one or two a day in advance.

Mike had been campaigning for an office job and in June, 1998, he was promoted to Captain of the Port (manager of all tug crews) and I took over as captain on the *Catherine Quigg*. Dave Gore who had just been hired came on as mate. Dave had quite a bit of experience in the towboat industry with most of it in management. Both Dave and Larry, the deckhand-engineer, were easy going which made for a good crew.

We occasionally had a trip to one of the refineries at Anacortes or Ferndale. On these trips a fourth man is added to the crew and we went on shifts of 6 hours on and 6 hours off. One of these trips was quite memorable. We were headed for the refinery at Ferndale when we ran into a hurricane force wind in Rosario Strait.

I was in bed sound asleep when the deckhand on watch woke me up and said that Dave needed help in the wheelhouse. That's when I noticed that the boat was starting to jump around. We had just rounded Tide Point on Cypress Island, in the San Juan Islands, and ran into a wind blowing 70 to 80 knots out of the northeast against a strong flood tide. It was a battle just to get to the wheelhouse. As I passed through the galley I saw the deckhand sitting on the floor with his back against a cupboard and his feet braced against the refrigerator door to keep it closed. He had a wastepaper basket in his lap because he was getting seasick. When I opened the door leading to the stairway up to the wheelhouse I found the waves had rearranged the furniture. The stairs were plugged with everything that had been loose in the wheelhouse. There was a stool, several charts, some books, magazines and coats. When I finally waded through the debris I found Dave with one hand on the steering wheel and one on the throttle. He was adjusting the speed when large waves hit us.

He asked me if I could determine our position. It was pitch black out and the air was full of water, from both rain and spray, so the radar didn't work and the spotlight was also useless. Dave knew there was a large oil tanker approaching from the stern and he was concerned that we had been pushed out into their path by the wind and tide. I pried the side door open enough to get a look around, was able to spot two familiar navigation lights and determined we were in the correct position. Because the tide was going with us we managed to make our way to the lee side of Lummi Island and out of the heavy swell.

We spent the morning there with the wind coming over the island in gusts of over 100 mph at times. Those were the strongest winds I had ever encountered. I was busy taking pictures of the strange sights of the wind gusts hitting the water as they roared down the steep side of the island. It was like a huge hand hitting the water making water fly in all directions and causing the boat to shake and rattle. I found out later that my entire picture taking episode had been for nothing. In my haste I had forgotten to put film in the camera!

Our office told us if we couldn't get to our destination by 2200 we would have to head back to Seattle empty, so we decided to make an attempt at getting into the dock. When we arrived off the refinery dock the wind was blowing 50 knots and the temperature had dropped below freezing, so now we had a coat of ice on everything. By dumping buckets of hot water on the tow winch we got it to work. Larry was splashed by waves while operating the tow winch and was covered with ice by the time he had finished pulling in the tow wire. When Dave climbed up on the barge after getting it alongside it was also covered with a sheet of ice. When he was standing still the wind was strong enough to slide him along the surface of the barge.

We had managed to get to the dock without doing any damage; by the time the barge was loaded the wind had dropped off and we had a comfortable trip back to Seattle.

Tugboat Life (1998 to 2006)
Chapter 45
Willapa Bay Job Begins

On the first of July, 1998, I was surprised by a request to attend a meeting at our company office in Seattle. It included people from three companies; Quigg Brothers, Olympic Tug and Barge and JJM, a Canadian company. I learned this was the job I was originally hired to do. The gathering was to distribute information to all the participants for a job beginning on July 5th, to build an underwater jetty at the mouth of Willapa Bay on the Washington coast.

The jetty was northwest of Tokeland, Washington, at Washaway Beach. The beach in this area was under attack from the ocean swell which had been gobbling up land at a fearful pace for many years. The theory was that the jetty would create a large sand bar that would protect the beach. The job had to be accomplished during the good weather months from July to September.

Quigg Brothers supplied a crane barge and its crew, and Olympic supplied two tugs and crews and one flat deck barge. The Canadian company, JJM, suppled a tug and three dump barges. The Canadians did the loading of rock at Tokart Bay in Barkley Sound on the west coast of Vancouver Island. Our job was to deliver the loaded barges to Willapa Bay, cross the bar, and maneuver the barge into the correct position for dumping.

We crewed up July 5th in Seattle on the *Alyssa Ann* with a crew of four. The *Alyssa Ann* is a 107 foot tug with two 8 cylinder EMD diesel engines for 2100 hp. This was my first time on this boat. We left Seattle with a full load of fuel and groceries and headed for Tokart Bay at the northeast corner of Barkley Sound about 200 miles from Seattle on the west coast of Vancouver Island.

When we arrived, the JJM crew had a loaded dump barge ready to go. These barges were self dumping. They were hinged at the top and an onboard engine opened up the bottom to dump the load. After the load was dumped it closed up again. All this was accomplished with a remote control from the tug. The barge was 160 feet long, 50 feet wide and drew 15 feet of water when loaded with 2500 tons of rock. This also meant it would jump up 15 feet when it dumped its load. The rock was from an old copper mine and was chosen because it was extremely hard and would endure the pounding of ocean waves for many years.

We hooked up and got underway. It was 24 hours one-way. The next day we arrived off the entrance of Willapa Bay and were met by the tug *James T. Quigg*. She was our pilot/guide for this first crossing of the bar. The channel was unmarked, had shallow water on both sides and swept through S turns making it extra challenging. Not to mention the ocean swell. It all made for an interesting crossing. The beach was so low laying it didn't produce a good radar target for navigation so we relied on GPS. After we made that first trip we produced an accurate GPS track that we could follow on future transits.

Upon arrival at the dump site the *James T. Quigg* hooked on to the stern of the barge and we tight-lined the barge (each tug pulling in the opposite direction) into position. This was not at all like being alongside a dock. We were in open water and needed to be within a few feet of the correct dump spot. We had to deal with some current and some swell. The jetty was being built in 60 feet of water. It all went something like this on the radio. "Ok, we are getting close, 20 more feet toward the beach. Ok 5 feet towards the ocean, move forward another 10 feet. Ok, that's it. Dump her." The positioning was done by a third small vessel that was alongside the barge with the use of GPS. Later on some of the dumps would be from alongside the crane barge.

After dumping our load we headed back to Tokart Bay with the empty barge for another load. The round trips were about 48 hours and we were at this for the next couple of months.

The second tug from Olympic was the *Lela Joy,* 77.5 length over all, with two V16-149 GMC diesel engines for 2200 hp. My job was to be the relief captain, while the other two captains worked two weeks on and one week off. I was relieving one captain for a week, and then switching boats to relieve the other captain for a week. After that I took a week off.

This was all new to me but I managed to sail though the first "bar crossing" and "barge dumping" with no problems and in record time - which put me in good standing with the job supervisor. Things were going well.

Tug *Alyssa Ann*

Tugboat Life (1998 to 2006)
Chapter 46
Willapa Bay Job Problems

We were making a round trip about every 48 hours to Tokart Bay and back to Willapa Bay. I stayed on the *Alyssa Ann* for one week then Captain Jeff Rickard came on to replace me and I went home for a week. A week later we loaded up a whole crew in a company car at Pier 23 in Seattle and headed for Tokeland (at the mouth of Willapa Bay on the Washington coast) to relieve the crew of the *Lela Joy*. We were going to have some problems that could be attributed to being new to the equipment. There was a learning curve to get through.

When we arrived at Tokeland our crew loaded onto the tug *James T. Quigg* for taxi service to the *Lela Joy*. The crew on the *Lela* had been on for two weeks and was used to working one week on and one week off so they were more than ready to get off. They had shortened their tow wire and were waiting for us inside the entrance to Willapa Bay. We had about two miles to run to get to them.

As soon as they saw us coming, they sped up to shorten the distance. They forgot to tighten down the brake on the tow winch and as soon as they accelerated the tow wire started to peel off the drum and they didn't notice it. Before they saw it, it all went overboard. 2500 feet of 1 ¾ inch wire went to the bottom.

Our first chore was to retrieve the wire so that meant the other crew was not going home until this had been accomplished. The procedure was to disconnect the wire from the barge and wind it on the tow winch backwards, and then we secured the outer end on the boat and wound the whole wire on back overboard. We attached the end still on the boat to the tow winch and wound it back aboard the proper way. It sounds easy, but it's not. The wire is heavy and awkward to handle. It took 5 or 6 hours.

We finally got underway and made a round trip every 48 hours. Each load was about 2750 tons of rock.

After part of the jetty was built out from the beach, a tug from Tacoma, the *Judy M.,* arrived with a flat barge loaded with larger rock. The flat barge was tied alongside the crane barge and with the use of the crane the crane crew started to cap the jetty, placing the larger rock on top of the smaller rock. This was all under water. The only place you could see the jetty was where it came off the beach. From that point on the top was 30 to 40 feet under water.

On the second trip, as we were crossing the bar on our way into Willapa Bay the steering quit. I called the captain of the *James T. Quigg,* who was at the work site and informed him of our problem. He headed out to help. There was about a 5 or 6 foot swell running and I was using the two engines to try to keep going straight but was not doing so well and had soon drifted out of the channel into shallow water. About this time I discovered that I had hit the wrong switch for manual steering and my problem was *operator* error. I turned the steering back on and after freeing the tow wire that was hung up on a sand bar we managed to re-enter the channel without the need of help from the *James T. Quigg*. That was an embarrassing error.

I was scheduled to switch boats after one week. As that time approached it became apparent that there would be a 36 hour layover between boats so I made arrangements to stay at the Tokeland Hotel. My wife came down and we made a mini vacation out of it, on the company's tab. The Tokeland Hotel is a Bed and Breakfast, over 100 years old. We had a good time and went beach combing at North Cove. This was in the area of the job site so I got a look at our operation from the beach side.

That afternoon the *Alyssa Ann* arrived and I got onboard. The crews on the *Alyssa* were having their own problems. One of the barges had a weak battery so on the southbound trips with a load; they were using the remote control to start the engine on the barge to charge the battery for a couple of hours. When they started this procedure, the remote had been left in the wrong sequence after the last dump. The next time the engine started the remote control automatically dumped the load of rocks out in the middle of the ocean. This resulted in the loss of 2700 tons of rock and some embarrassment for the crew. It was also the end of using the remote controls. Everything would be done manually from then on. The rest of my week on the *Alyssa Ann* went smoothly and I was soon off for another week.

Lela Joy

Tugboat Life (1998 to 2006)
Chapter 47
Lela Joy sinks

The wind and sea was calm through July and August with some larger swells at times. There were low clouds and fog almost every morning that would last into the afternoon and sometimes stay with us all day.

From July to mid September I was on a "2 week on/1 week off" schedule - then everything changed!

On the second week in September, I was on my week off. A couple of days before it was time for me to go back I tried to call the *Lea Joy* to arrange the time for me to come back aboard.

After a couple of days and several tries I was still unable to make contact so I called the other tug on the job to see if they could help me. I got ahold of Captain Rickard on my first try and the first words out of his mouth were, "Haven't you heard?" "Haven't I heard what?" I said. "The *Lela Joy* has sunk!" "SUNK WHERE? Is everybody okay?" Jeff explained to me that the crew on the *Lela Joy* had been taking on fuel at Raymond, Washington. The engineer and the captain had decided to try to make her ride better by loading her down heavy with fuel, water, lube oil and filling an extra unused tank with more water.

The captain was on the dock talking to someone while a hose from a fuel truck on the dock was filling the last empty fuel tank. The engineer and a dock-side mechanic had just come up out of the engine room for a drink of water and the mate was tending the fuel hose on the boat.

The boat suddenly rolled to port against the dock. The dock mechanic dashed up the stairs to the wheelhouse and out onto the upper deck. At the same time, the engineer ran to the back engine room hatch in an effort to close it, while the mate ran up to the bow. Both the mate and dock mechanic were able to jump off onto the dock as the boat rolled over on its left side. The engineer lost the race to close the back hatch and had to go overboard under the dock. The water rushed in through the back hatch and the boat sank to the bottom in about 15 feet of water alongside the dock. This all happened very fast, in a few short minutes.

There were a few moments of panic as every one on the dock was trying to find out where the engineer had gone. Was he trapped under or inside the boat? A few minutes later he came walking up the beach at the end of the dock soaking wet. He had jumped overboard as the boat rolled and swam to the beach underneath the dock then walked out from under the dock. The boat ended up sitting somewhat upright with about half of the wheelhouse sticking out of the water.

This sudden rolling to port was caused by the empty tank they filled with water. It had no baffles; baffles are walls that create compartments in the tank with small openings that keep the fluid from shifting from side to side rapidly. Once the boat became overloaded it tipped over far enough that water entered the back hatch; that was the last straw.

The engineer called his wife to come and get him and he disappeared from that company forever. The captain got a ride home, packed his bags and headed for Mexico. I think they both assumed they would be fired and were probably worried they would be responsible for the damages.

After a few days the company brought in a crane and lifted the *Lela Joy* back to the surface. When they unhooked the crane she rolled over to the other side and sank again. On the next try they were able to keep her floating. She was delivered to a shipyard and everything was stripped out of the inside. She was completely rebuilt over several months to the tune of about a million dollars.

The crew on the *Alyssa Ann* decided to stay on for the rest of the job that would last a few more weeks so I thought I was out of a job. After a few days I was called back to work as captain on the *Catherine Quigg*. The same boat I had been working on prior to July 5th, pulling oil barges around Puget Sound.

Tugboat Life (1998 to 2006)
Chapter 48
Back on *Catherine Quigg*
Move to *Lela Joy*

Working at Olympic Tug & Barge on the *Catherine Quigg* in Tacoma and Seattle harbors became routine, fueling the same ships as they arrived at various docks on their regular schedules. We were based in Tacoma and under contract to US Oil. US Oil has a terminal with two docks on the Blair Waterway in Tacoma.

This work was time sensitive. While waiting for the next job we stood by at Dock #2, and then shifted the barge over to Dock #1 to load the product just in time to make it to the ship. The bunker fuel was loaded aboard the barge at about 150 degrees and immediately begins to cool. The hotter the product the better it flowed through the pump. We needed to get it completely discharged before it dropped below 90 degrees which took about 36 hours.

For harbor work we ran a three man crew; captain, mate and deckhand-engineer and worked one week on and one week off. The jobs varied from one or two deliveries a day to dry spells with no jobs for one or two days. We used these slow times to catch up on boat and barge maintenance and rest.

Once or twice a month we were sent off on jobs outside the US Oil contract. One of these jobs was hauling sand and gravel for Concrete Tech, a company that produced concrete constructions beams. Their dock was also on the Blair Waterway right beside US Oil. The gravel pit was at DuPont south of Tacoma through the Tacoma Narrows. We hooked up and pushed the barge ahead for the entire trip. This involved positioning the bow of the tug in the exact center of the stern of the barge, and then running lines each direction to the corners of the barge to keep the bow in position. Then running two lines from each stern quarter, one tied down and the other one attached to the stern winch to be able to tighten up the hook-up so the tug was lined up exactly down the center line of the barge. This transforms the barge into becoming part of the tug and it is possible to drive it around like a boat.

Upon arrival at the DuPont dock we attached two cables, one at each end of the barge that the dock crew used to move the barge along as they loaded it.

The sand and gravel is delivered by long conveyer belts that run from the pit to the dock and through a pipe suspended over the barge. The gravel pit crew loaded the barge in about two hours.

Every effort was made to schedule the trips to DuPont on the correct tidal current, flood tide for going down to DuPont and ebb tide for coming back. The current in the area of the Tacoma Narrows Bridge can run about 5 knots. If we were going against this amount of current our progress would be mighty slow. Going with the current our trips were about 4 hours down and 6 hours back with 1000 tons of sand and gravel.

I was biding my time on the *Catherine Quigg* waiting for the chance to move to a larger tug. The opportunity came along when the company purchased the *Pacific Falcon* in 1999. She was 121 feet long with 4000 horsepower. After a short period of orientation I was ready to take over as captain. On that day there was some kind of dispute within the management group. One of the managers took over as captain and I was back on the *Catherine Quigg*. This was somewhat disappointing to me but I was fairly new in this company and felt powerless to influence these decisions.

The next chance came along when the tug *Lela Joy* was through with her rebuild after her sinking at Raymond, Washington. Dave, the mate who was working with me, had come from a management job in another company and had been campaigning for an office position. Rumor had it that Dave would be getting the captain's job on the *Lela Joy* so I let it be known that I would be unhappy with that and lo-and-behold I got the job. Dave moved to captain of the *Lucy Franco* and after some time got his management job.

The *Lela Joy* had a million dollar rebuild with all new interior and new engines. It was quiet in the wheelhouse and she had a fairly good ride in bad weather. I would be on her for the next two years until the economy slowed down and consequently so did the oil business.

Tugboat Life (1998 to 2006)
Chapter 49
Move to tug *Alyssa Ann*

I was crewed up on the *Lela Joy* and we were tied to a dock in Seattle when the port captain came aboard for a chat. This was not unusual but it usually meant something was up. There was going to be some shifting around of crew members to different boats. Some people might be laid off and a boat or two might be tied up because of a slow down in business. He told me I could have what ever boat I wished to be on. I assumed I had proven myself and was in good standing in the company.

We discussed different options and I decided that the tug *Alyssa Ann* and the barge *Norton,* which was under contract to Tesoro Oil Company, was the most stable job in the company. After one week off, I was on the *Alyssa Ann* with a 4 man crew, a mate and 2 deckhand-tankermen and an engineer.

The mate, Larry Gladsjo, had been a logger and moved to tug boating when business slowed down. Ken Olsen, one of the deckhand/tanker men, developed an internet company and moved to tug boating after selling his company. Brandon Shafie, the other deckhand-tankerman, had followed his father into the tugboat business.

Bob Mack the engineer had an interesting past. He tried king crab fishing one season and came back owing the company money. After some thought, he decided to give it another try and came back after that season with $80,000.00 dollars in his pocket and was hooked. After a few seasons Bob became captain on his own fishing boat. This was during the golden age of crab fishing when big money was being made in Alaska.

Being gone fishing 9 or 10 months of the year did not go well with married life and in time Bob decided to change careers. We had been working together for several months when Bob told me he had expected to have a captain's job on a tug after a short time. He was surprised that running a tug and barge was so much more complicated than a fishing boat. He never did reach his goal and died in a river swimming accident in Eastern Washington trying to save two other swimmers.

The *Alyssa Ann,* at 93.7 feet long and 27 feet wide, drew 14 feet of water. It had 2100 horse power from 2 EMD 8 cylinder diesel engines that swung two, 73 inch four bladed stainless steel propellers inside fixed Kort nozzles[9]. The *Alyssa* was built in 1966 at Golden Meadow, Los Angeles, California. At the deck level were three state rooms with bunks for 8 people, a head and shower and the galley. The next level up had the captain's room and private head, also a chart room with three steps up to the wheelhouse. There was a control station at the back of the upper deck for controlling the boat and running the tow winch.

---

[9] A cylinder around the propeller

She was an old boat but I found her quite comfortable, a little too noisy in the galley, but very quiet in the wheelhouse, where I spent most of my time.

The barge *Norton*, 271x76 feet, has a load capacity of 42,000 barrels of bunker fuel that is 1,764,000 gallons and 2500 barrels of diesel, or 105,000 gallons. The Norton was built in 1950 and was originally used to haul asphalt to Hawaii. It was down 14.5 feet in the water fully loaded. It had a heating system onboard to keep the bunker fuel hot with a burner that heated peanut oil and circulated it through a piping system that runs through the tanks. The tankermen would fire up the diesel powered burner when ever the oil fell below 100 degrees or just before the next delivery. The barge also has a computer-run blending system which was added later that mixes bunker fuel and diesel to the correct blend for the customer and delivers it to the ship.

Normally we went to the Tesoro Refinery Dock at Anacortes and filled up the barge then returned to Seattle to fuel ships. In between jobs we tied at Pier 48 and took care of maintenance on the tug and barge. The deckhand/tankermen managed the loading and unloading of the barge and blending the product. I and the engineer and the mate took care of the boat, including the maintenance and most of the wheel watches underway. At times we all worked on what ever was needed on the barge or the boat. This included washing the tug or the barge with soap and water and chipping and painting both vessels.

The *Alyssa Ann* was a little low on horse power for handling a barge this large so we had to keep on our toes or things got out of control. When pushing alongside, stern first, fully loaded, you needed to keep the speed lower than 3 knots or the barge would start to shear off and head in a different direction.

A short time after we got into a routine with loading in Anacortes and discharging in Seattle or Tacoma, word came down that we would be moving to the Columbia River for work in the Portland, Oregon, and Vancouver, Washington, area in the summer of 2001.

Another crew moved the tug and barge down while we were on our time off and on our next crew up we had to drive down to Portland. We crew-changed at a terminal on the Willamette River, then my crew loaded the barge and did one discharge to a ship. That turned out to be the end of our work on the Columbia River; management sent us back to Seattle.

Next, along came September 11, 2001, and Homeland Security. Things got a little tense for awhile. It was thought that oil barges might be a target of terrorists and new regulations were added to an already heavily regulated business. We would need to have a 24 hour watch over our barges and be moored in a secure area. These regulations included all flood lights on at night and nobody allowed aboard without preauthorization from our office.

Alyssa Ann and barge *Norton*

Approach to go alongside ship for fueling

Tugboat Life (1998 to 2006)
Chapter 50
Relieved of Duty

Life on the *Alyssa Ann* was good with a crew that got along well together, but I was soon to experience the political side of tug boating. I found out that I needed to be careful when dealing with the port captain.

With work slowing down management started sending people home if their tug had no work. My crew and I were sent home with the word that we would not be coming back for the rest of our shift. At home I asked my wife if she would like to go on a road trip to the ocean since I had about ten days off. We loaded up and headed out. We were about half way to our destination when I got a call that we were going back to work. My response was, "sorry, I was told there would be no work and I have left for a trip."

I went back to work on my next shift. We were coming back from Anacortes with a loaded barge headed to Seattle when we got a call from the office that we were to tie up the barge and I was to pick two people to stay aboard to watch the equipment. I broke the news to the crew. One of the deckhand-engineers told me he had a bad case of athlete's foot and would like to get off and use sick leave. I relayed this information to the port captain and I think he thought I was trying to keep this man on the payroll.

Because of my experience with the last layoff I decided to call the Tesoro dispatcher to get an idea of how long we would be off. I soon got a call from our port captain and he stated that as soon as we were tied up he wanted the entire crew to come to the office. What I didn't know then was that the Tesoro dispatcher had called our port captain and stated that she wished they would not layoff the boat because Tesoro was paying to have it fully crewed all the time. I was about to find out that this seriously pissed him off.

After arriving at the office we were ushered into the conference room. When the port captain arrived he read us the riot act and stated that we were employed by Olympic Tug and Barge and not Tesoro and we were not to discuss Olympic business with them. He then picked the two men to stay onboard the boat and told the rest of the crew to go home, and told me to stick around.

As soon as the crew had left the room he told me that I was relieved of duty and I was to go home and wait until they decided what to do with me. I asked if I could get my gear off the boat and he said I could. When I got down to the boat and told the crew what had happened they were shocked. I was still confused. I think it could have been a combination of things, partly the request for sick leave for the deckhand, a slow down in business that had put pressure on management, things that had happened to the crew before I moved aboard, and somebody having a bad day.

I went home and spent a week worrying about my fate. I expected their call eventually. I finally got the call to come back for a meeting. I sat in front of a three person board in the company conference room, Olympics vice president, port captain and the port captain of Harley Marine, the parent company of Olympic Tug and Barge. The Harley Marine port captain was the moderator. He brought up all the incidents I had been involved in since coming to the company. He included the crunching of the corner of the dock at Pier 48 that had already been destroyed before I got to it, but because I set off a fire sprinkler and alarm a bill for $100,000.00 was sent to the company from the port.

Also, I and a crew had been sent to California to deliver a tug and barge to the Columbia River. Halfway between L.A. and San Francisco we had a main engine die so we limped into San Francisco. We tied the barge up and took the tug back to Seattle for repairs. The barge was delivered to Portland by another company in a storm and sustained $250,000 damage. That cost went on my record along with the cost of the engine repairs to the tune of $500,000. I had heard that when the tug's engines were repaired it was found that they were virtually dead and just happened to die completely on my watch. All these things together made me look like the worst captain in the company. The irony of the whole thing is I was reassigned to another of their tugs doing the exact same work for Olympic hauling Tesoro Oil.

Departing from a cruise ship "bunkering" with a barge "on the hip".

Tugboat Life (1998 to 2006)
Chapter 51
Move to *Lucy Franco*
Fueling Cruise Ships

I was reassigned to the tug *Lucy Franco*. Like the *Alyssa Anne*, it was under contract to Tesoro. Our main job was bunkering ships. Occasionally we would be sent, to assist other tugs with oil barges, or to move construction barges or to setting out anchors.

The *Lucy Franco* was 69 feet x 26 feet and drew 10 feet of water. She had two Caterpillar diesel engines for a total of 1250 horsepower and was built in 1981 at Providence, Rhode Island. She had a fairly large galley for her size. The crew's quarters were down below and toward the bow. The captain's room was on the second deck behind the wheelhouse.

I had a new crew of fairly inexperienced young men, a mate and two deckhand-engineers. We got along well which made for a good work experience. We were working a week on and a week off in the Seattle and Tacoma area.

But for me this was a confusing situation - I had been: 1) relieved of duty, 2) sent home, 3) made to appear before a three man board, 4) convicted of ? (I'm still not sure what), then 5) sent back to work doing the same thing I'd been doing before all this occurred.

At this time we received a new set of rules when doing jobs for Tesoro. Instead of receiving our job orders directly from Tesoro dispatch they were sent to Olympic dispatch and then Olympic sent them to us.

Olympic Tug and Barge had contracts for almost all the ship bunkering on Puget Sound. The only other company in the business was Foss. On December 30, 2003, Foss had a large oil spill, caused by operator error, at the asphalt terminal at Point Wells just north of Seattle. The result of that spill was that Foss got out of the black oil business. At about the same time cruise ship arrivals in Seattle were increasing and Olympic Tug and Barge got their fueling business.

The cruise ships arrived in Seattle on weekends. We were using a barge that hauled both bunker fuel and diesel because most of the cruise ships used both. They burned bunker fuel which was less expensive out in the open ocean. Bunker fuel burned dirty and created more pollution: diesel was burned when entering inland waters. We filled up the barge either at Point Wells or at the refinery dock at Anacortes on Thursday or Friday and fueled one cruise ship on Saturday morning and one on Sunday morning. Between jobs we tied up, usually at Pier 23 or Pier 90 in Seattle. Pier 23 is in the East Waterway right next to the West Seattle low level bridge and Pier 90 is at the north end of the harbor.

The cruise ships arrived in Seattle between 0530 - 0600 both mornings. The business increased to three ships arriving on each day, two at Pier 30 and one at Pier 66. These ships entered the harbor in a convoy after running all night at the correct speed to arrive at the exact time every trip. Because three ships arrived simultaneously, it took three Olympic Tug and Barge barges to supply the service.

Timing was important for these jobs as were all of our fueling jobs. We timed our arrival alongside the ship at an open door just above the water line at 0800. An Olympic Tug and Barge tankerman came aboard with us before we left the dock for the job. Olympic had a group of shore-based tankermen who came aboard only to load and unload the barges. The tug crew secured the barge to the ship with four mooring lines and assisted the tankerman moving the six inch heavy fuel hose aboard the ship with the use of the crane on the barge.

To protect the pretty white ship, we draped white canvas over the black bumper tires and tried to land very gently alongside. There was always a group of on-lookers on the passenger deck. It was a quick way to lose your captain's job if you bumped too hard or marked up one of those ships.

The tankerman pumped aboard on average about 300 tons which is 2000 barrels or 84,000 gallons of bunker 380 fuel. Some of the ships would also take a few hundred barrels of diesel. These cruise ship jobs took 5 or 6 hours. After the tankerman was through with the discharge and the paperwork, we helped him load the hose back aboard the barge and returned to our dock to await the next morning's job.

During the rest of the week we bunkered other container or cargo ships or worked with construction companies. One of my favorite jobs was working with a construction company at the submarine base at Bangor, Washington, in Hood Canal. Hood Canal is the long narrow stretch of water that separates the mainland from the Olympic Peninsula.

To transit through Hood Canal we contacted the Hood Canal floating bridge 24 hours ahead of time to make an appointment to have the bridge opened if we were towing something with a high mast. If we were running light or had a low lying barge we used the high rise at either end of the bridge.

One of the transits through the open bridge turned out to be a white knuckle affair. As I approached the bridge with a tall-masted crane barge I called the operator on VHF radio and he asked me if I needed both sides open giving me 200 feet of room. My thought was I didn't need all that room and told him one-half would be enough. The barge was 35 feet wide which gave me 30 feet clearance on each side. That turned out to be a near disaster. I shortened the tow wire to 30 feet and headed through. As I entered the opening the wind suddenly picked up from the east and shoved the barge to the side. It moved sideways toward the closed swing span. I gave the engine full power and held my breath and we managed to clear the bridge by about 10 feet. If I had hit the bridge it probably would have put the bridge out of commission, closing a major highway to the Olympic Peninsula, for who knows how long.

We also contacted Bangor security several hours ahead of our arrival to inform them we were coming and to open the floating fence that surrounded the base. Once inside we would help move equipment, crane barges, and shift their mooring anchors. It was always interesting work.

Lucy Franco

PART – IV
Tugboat Life (2006 to 2010)
Chapter 52
Pacific Northwest Marine Services

Life on the *Lucy Franco* was working out well but I was keeping my distance from the office as much as possible. After the incident of getting relieved from duty off the *Alyssa Anne* I had decided to keep my eye out for a chance to move to another company.

Steve, a mate and engineer I had worked with on several occasions, had resigned from Olympic to help start a new company. Steve's good friend and school mate was going to purchase the tug *Anne Carlander* and haul scrap metal from the Fraser River in British Columbia, Canada to Tacoma. I had talked to him several times and stated that if they ever needed another captain I might be interested.

Then one day when I was on my time off I got a call from Steve that they needed me for one trip that day. They had crashed a barge into a marina in Tacoma and the Coast Guard inspector had discovered that the mate's license was not valid for that job and he was not allowed to sail until the license was updated.

Olympic's rules allowed for work outside the company as long as it was not a competing business, so I took the trip. This was the chance I needed to get acquainted with the owner, David Joseph.

Then, just after Christmas in 2005, I got a call from David. He had given his crew on the *Anne Carlander* time off between Christmas and New Year, then a job came up. When he asked them to come back they held him to his time off promise. He asked me if I could come up with a crew and make the trip. I was on my time off again so I found two deckhands and David, the owner, went as mate.

A few months passed and I got another call from Steve. He asked if I could give David a call. I did and he said his captain was resigning and he wanted to know if I was interested in coming to work for them full time. We arranged to meet for lunch in Seattle and talk it over.

Lunch was at Salty's in West Seattle with just David and me. We discussed the terms of my employment. I needed to give Olympic at least two weeks notice and I asked that David provide health insurance that equaled what I had at Olympic. I also mentioned that if I quit Olympic right then I would be losing out on about $ 6000.00 in vacation pay and sick leave benefits. David agreed to my terms and offered to pay a $ 6000.00 signing bonus. We shook hands on it and David asked me to research health plans and find one that was satisfactory. I found a broker in Burlington that could supply the right plan and referred him to David.

The next time I went to work at Olympic Tug and Barge I turned in the paperwork for two week's notice of my resignation. I felt bad in that I was handing this to a new, just- hired port captain but explained to him that my resignation was the result of events that occurred prior to him taking the job.

I went back out to the tug and within a short time I got a call to come back into the office. It had been decided that if I were resigning it would have to be immediately. That was fine with me, in fact I had expected it. I said goodbye to everybody, gathered up all my gear from the tug and headed home. As soon as I got home I called David and told him I was ready to go to work when they needed me. In a few days I was off to work for Pacific Marine Northwest Services on the tug *Anne Carlander*.

Anne Carlander on the beach at Port Townsend Shipyard

Tugboat life (2006 to 2010)
Chapter 53
Starting to Work on
Anne Carlander

The tug *Anne Carlander* was like an old friend. By 2006 I had made hundreds of trips on her on the inland waters of Puget Sound and British Columbia. She was 69 feet on the keel, 75 ft over all, 23 feet wide and drew 13.5 feet when fully loaded.[10] The main engine turned a 72 inch, 4 bladed stainless propeller inside a steerable Kort nozzle, which confined the water flow in a tube past the propeller, which increases the horsepower by about 10%. The steer-able nozzle is the rudder and creates a very positive effect on thrust and steering in both forward and reverse.

Pacific Northwest Marine Services (PNMS) was owned by David Joseph and his wife Marcie of Gig Harbor, Washington. The four-man crew consisted of Steve as First Captain and Chief Engineer, me as Second Captain, Luke as Deckhand/ engineer/ cook, and a second deckhand position that was filled by several different people over time. Dave had other people he could call to relieve a person on the crew for a trip, if needed.

---

[10] Her main engine was a 1100 horse Cat D-399, V-16 cylinder diesel engine and for Auxiliary power two D-330 Cat diesels with generators attached.

In most tug companies the crew consists of a captain and a mate. Steve and I traded watches every trip and shared the captain's job. Whoever was on shift during barge maneuvering or landing or departures acted as captain. In other companies a normal shift is 6 to 12 and 12 to 6, but we ran our shifts from, 8 to 2 and 2 to 8, six hours on and six off. The crew stood 6 hour watches and everybody was up for most arrivals and departures. The two deckhands took care of the machinery and cooked lunch and dinner. Breakfast was every man for himself.

Our main business was hauling barges for Amix Salvages and Sales Ltd., of Surrey, British Columbia, to Schnitzer Steel in the Hylebos Waterway in Tacoma. When I started, Amix had four 200 by 60 foot barges, with a hauling capacity of 2000 ton each. They had a yard along the Fraser River at Surrey, B.C., just above the bridges at New Westminster. We hauled empty barges northbound and loaded ones southbound. We had the equipment to haul three barges at one time in a tandem tow. The first year I worked we hauled 95 loaded barges to Tacoma. The next year our biggest we moved 113 loaded barges to Tacoma. In later years we hauled fewer loads but we started using larger barges which held heavier loads. Those larger barges were 235 by 60 feet wide and could haul up to about 3000 ton.

Departing Fraser River with two small barges in tow. (notice how 2nd barge is not visible)

Departing Tacoma with three empty barges in tow

Back in the day Amix Salvage would have been called a junkyard but as recycling became viable and profitable things changed. Amix had a machine that crushed cars down to 3 feet high. Amix loaded the barges at their dock with a mobile crane that picked up an entire car with a large hand-like clamp and swing it on to the barge. The loads consisted of all types of metal, including crushed cars, used appliances, dismantled machinery, and wire cable. We once had an entire load of Vancouver, B.C., city buses headed for the recycling.

Sea Link Yarder 330 x 60, cargo deck as big as a foot ball field. For size comparison notice the man in yellow raincoat standing on bow just behind the name of the barge

The Amix dock was 500 yards above the railroad swing bridge at New Westminster. This location made for interesting arrivals and departures, especially departures. The current ran over 5 knots during the spring run off. If the current was running at a pretty good clip on departure we hooked up the barge with our wire bridles and pulled it up the river a half mile to get room to turn around and straightened up before we arrived at the bridge. This was important because the current pushed us hard down stream, sweeping us through the bridge at 5 knots. There were a few occasions we waited for the current to slow down before we departed.

The railroad bridge is a swing bridge and is set at an angle to the current. The outbound traffic uses the south opening. I held away from the center span and timed our speed so we were dead center in the opening when we got there. The current pushes directly towards the center wall. We usually used an assist tug when transiting with the larger barges. If done just right there was about 30 feet of clearance on both sides. If done wrong we could tear down a portion of the wood sidewalls in the opening. That meant a Coast Guard investigation and a very large expense for our company. We saw that a couple of times over the years, when other tugs missed their timing and lineup. The other two bridges at the same location are high-rise and don't require an opening.

For a two barge tandem tow an assist tug took the second barge through the bridges and brought it to us to hookup on the fly below the bridges. The assist tug took the second barge down first and we followed him. After clearing the bridges we slowed down and dropped out 500 feet of tow wire until the hook-up link was in the middle of the back deck. Then we hooked up another set of tow bridles. The assist tug lead the second barge up to our stern with his deckhand on the barge who took our bridles and hooked them up to the barge while at the same time disconnecting their bridles. This took the entire crew to accomplish; one man to run the tug, two men to handle the bridles and the fourth man to watch for other traffic as we were being swept along with the current.

Sometimes we had three barges to take to Tacoma but we were allowed to tow only two barges in the Fraser River. This required another tug to bring the third barge down to the mouth of the river and hand it off to us. Our normal tow was two small barges or one large barge, but we did tow three barges a few times over the years.

Hooking up second set of bridles

Second barge hooked up

Tugboat Life (2006 to 2010)
Chapter 54
Scrap Metal and Marijuana Discovery

When I went to work on the *Anne Carlander* the scrap metal market was starting to boom. Prices were rising and steel was pouring into the recycling yards. We were busy hauling loads between Canada and Tacoma.

At the Amix yard at Surrey, B.C., the truck loads of arriving scrap metal were lined up at the entrance gate. The trucks were weighed, unloaded, and the metal was stacked in piles according to grade. There were several different grades from crushed cars, mixed metal, cast iron up to the top grade that could go directly to the smelter without sorting. This was a hectic place, with trucks arriving with loads and barges being loaded in the same area. Large, off-road trucks drove right onto the barge by the use of a ramp and dumped their loads. A mobile crane stacked the load high, crushed cars around the edges and loose metal in the center. As the space on the barge filled the crane moved back to the dock, picked the scrap off the trucks and swung it onto the barge to finish off the load.

Most of the time when we arrived with an empty barge, there was a loaded barge waiting to depart. Paperwork was exchanged and we were underway in about 30 minutes. This was not always the case. Sometimes we had to wait for the barge to be loaded and occasionally we spent the night. Most of our round trips were 48 hours.

Below: The beginning of a load.
Above: Just about finished loading.

Our office did the necessary reporting to US Customs and Immigration and a customs brokerage in Seattle took care of the paperwork. The Amix's office took care of the Canadian reporting and paperwork.

Just before I went to work on the *Ann Carlander* the crew had found several large sports bags of marijuana hidden on one of the loaded barges. The new deckhand had placed the stern light on the barge in the wrong place and when the mate was retrieving the light after arriving in Tacoma he noticed the bags. They reported this to the Coast Guard and later wished they had just thrown them overboard. They were treated like criminals. The Coast Guard and Police came aboard with a dog and searched every space on the boat. Because the mate, Brian Adams, had touched the bags of marijuana the dog went nuts in his room and they proceeded to tear his room apart.

For the next year we were boarded and searched several times in Canada and the U.S. We were even boarded underway in the Fraser River when 8 customs officers and a dog came aboard from a launch. Nobody was ever arrested when the marijuana was discovered but the Yard Foreman at Amix was fired. The crew on the *Anne Carlander* had noticed that he had taken a special interest in their departure.

Much to our relief the close attention from customs faded away over time.

In Tacoma, we tied the loaded barges at a barge storage area in the harbor and proceeded to our dock to report to Customs. After Customs we locked the boat and went home until the next trip. Later, Foss harbor tugs shifted the loaded barges to the Schnitzer dock for unloading and moved the empty barges out to barge storage. When we came back to work the empties were waiting for us.

At Schnitzer, the unloaded scrap metal was piled on the dock. Everything got broken down. The crushed cars were sent through a machine that ground them into small chunks. Two or three times a month bulk carrier ships arrived and loaded up the metal and headed for China.

Tugboat Life (2006 to 2010)
Chapter 55
Barge Almost Sinks Underway

When I first looked at the Amix barges that we would be using I thought, "Oh boy, we are going to spend a lot of time checking these barges for water and pumping them out." They looked to be in pretty tough shape. What I didn't know then was that Amix had an excellent crew, equivalent to a shipyard, and the barges were being well maintained when they were tied to their dock. We never did have much trouble with the barges. I think we may have pumped a barge 2 or 3 times in five years. We were prepared anyway. We had a portable pump onboard the tug. We could also use the tug's bilge pump by using external hookups on the outside of the deckhouse and 100 feet of 4 inch suction hose stored on board.

3 AMIX barges in tow from Tacoma

All four barges were constructed with a steel wall on three sides and the bow open to facilitate loading with a ramp from the front. I wondered about these open bows in rough weather. Might they fill up the cargo area with water and destabilize? This actually was not a problem, except for a couple of times which I will tell about later.

I did have one trip when I thought the barge we were towing was going to sink or roll over. I was on the 2 AM to 8 AM watch and had just taken over from the other captain. We were rounding Point Partridge on Whidbey Island north of Port Townsend. The barge suddenly took a shear to the right and didn't want to come back straight. I turned the spotlight on it and noticed that it was riding low in the bow and had a starboard list. The weather had been calm so this could not have been from water slopping over the bow.

The barge was in danger of sinking or rolling over so I needed to get into deep water. If it did go over we wouldn't create a hazard to navigation. I called the Coast Guard and informed them of our situation. I didn't mention to them about getting into deep water, and they instructed us to hold our position. We slowed to an idle, kept an eye on the barge, and slowly moved into deeper water. After some time the barge didn't seem to be getting any worse. I asked the Coast Guard if I could continue underway to take advantage of the large flood tide that was starting to run in Admiralty Inlet. At first they refused my request but after several conversations and explaining that the further south we got the closer we would be to some help they allowed us to proceed south to Tacoma.

We had to run slowly or the water washed over the bow and onto the barge's deck. In the meantime our office was trying to arrange some help for us. After a few hours and some assistance from the flood tide we were in the area of Port Madison just north of Seattle when Steve, the port captain, arrived in a small boat with a couple of pumps. We inched into Port Madison and went alongside the barge. Because the cargo covered the hatch we had to cut a hole in the steel deck of the bow with a cutting torch and began to pump it out.

After about 4 hours we had most of the water pumped out, but we still didn't know where the water had come from. That's when we discovered a small hole about the size of your fist in the curve of the bow just above the water line. It was okay as long as we were not moving but as soon as we did a bow wake was produced and the water started pouring inside. Because of the small size of the hole it took several hours before it caused a problem. We informed the Coast Guard of our findings and they allowed us to continue on to Tacoma. Just another day in the life of a tugboater!

The hole was probably caused by a harbor tug at Surrey while shifting the barge into the dock for loading. Those small, 30 foot, tugs have lots of power and sometimes get ripping around in the river current with a barge in tow and get a little out of control.

Tugboat Life (2006 to 2010)
Chapter 56
Water in the Cargo Area

To look at those heavily loaded barges one might think they were unstable but they were not, even though the cargo was piled 15 to 20 feet high. Still we had to be careful about pulling them into rough weather. On a few occasions we had to wait in a sheltered area for the wind to die down. The main problem we ran into was water splashing over the bow and running into the cargo area. Normally the water ran right through and out the scupper holes in the stern or sides. On two trips those scuppers became plugged with debris from the scrap metal. The scrap metal was not nice and clean; some had probably been sitting around in junkyards for months or years and arrived with all kinds of dirt and garbage clinging to it. Some of this debris was knocked loose and ended up on the barge deck.

The first time we ran into trouble was in the Fraser River. We were headed outbound with the current and ran into a 25 knot northwest wind with 4 to 5 foot swells. Water was splashing over the bow and in about 30 minutes the barge started listing. I got in touch with Amix and they requested we come back to New Westminster harbor so they could check the barge. Upon arrival at the harbor a crew from Amix arrived in a small skiff and checked it over. The barge has scuppers, openings in the side walls at deck level, 1 foot high by 3 feet long. The Amix men poked steel rods in the scuppers to break an opening through the blockage and water poured out. We got under way again and made the rest of the trip without further incident.

The next time we had trouble with water, we were again exiting the Fraser River with a loaded barge. I had gone off shift and was in my bunk when I noticed the swell started lifting the boat. As I lay there for awhile and the motion increased I began to wonder if the guys in the wheelhouse were paying attention to the barge. I got up to check. As I started up the stairway to the wheelhouse I heard someone say, "Here he comes now."

We had hired another mate and he was on with me. He had left the two deckhands to watch things in the wheelhouse while he went to the galley to make a sandwich. When I looked at the barge it already had a dangerous port list. We were out of the river and in open water so at this point we had several options. We could slow down to stop the swell from breaking over the bow. We could change course to meet the swell at an angle. Or we could turn downwind and take a route through the sheltered water of Porlier Pass and the Gulf Islands.

The two men in the wheelhouse had not been paying close attention to the barge and before they knew it the barge had taken on water in the 5 or 6 foot swell and was starting to list.

I took over the controls, and slowed the boat to an idle and started a gentle turn to the right to head downwind. As the barge started to turn the list became more severe and we thought it was going to roll. Then a whole row of crushed cars on the port side peeled off and went overboard. This brought the barge back to a more stable position.

We were about an hour out of the Fraser River so all those cars were headed for the bottom of the Strait of Georgia in very deep water to make habitat for the fish. Those 60 to 80 crushed cars would stay there forever because they would be impossible to retrieve.

We headed downwind and through Porlier Pass and into calm waters. This was on Saturday but I finally got ahold of the manager at Amix and he asked us to head back up the river to Amix and they would replace the lost cargo with a new supply.

I don't remember what the price of scrap metal was at that time, but the loss of several tons and the time and labor to replace it, added up to a good sum of money.

Back through Porlier Pass and across the choppy water and up the river we went. We arrived back at Surrey about midnight. A blurry eyed Amix crew arrived Sunday morning to reload the barge.

I don't think there were any repercussions on our end of the operation. We had been warning Amix about the problem of plugged scuppers for quite a while. After that incident a front loading scraper was brought aboard each barge prior to loading and the scuppers were cleaned before loading. It solved the problem. We didn't have any more barges trying to roll over.

Tugboat Life (2006 to 2010)
Chapter 57
Storms between Tacoma and Fraser River

When transiting between Tacoma and the Fraser River the weather was always a concern. The worst area was always the Strait of Juan de Fuca. When crossing the straits with the west wind blowing, the swell was on our port side. There were very few times that we had to stop for weather north bound with empty barges, but several times we stopped with loaded barges southbound.

A couple of the north bound trips were memorable. On one we had rounded Point Partridge on Whidbey Island when the west wind started to blow. As we approached Lawson Reef at the entrance to Rosario Strait the wind had increased and the swell was 10 to 12 feet coming from the west. It was night and the waves were crashing against the port side. Spray was flying over the top of us and the boat was jumping around violently. To improve our situation we had slowed down and angled into the swell. This headed us northwest in an attempt to obtain a better course for crossing Lawson Reef. When we changed directions again conditions were only slightly better, but this kept us in the swell longer until we had worked our way far enough into Rosario Strait where we finally got out of the swell.

Usually empty barges were not much of a worry, but I was always concerned about breaking the bridles or the tow wire. We had been beat up badly by the waves for about two hours and it was a big relief, like a heavy weight taken off my shoulders, when we were back in calm water unscathed.

On another northbound trip I was off shift when we encountered strong wind and large swells off Point Wilson north of Port Townsend. David, the owner who was relieving the other captain for this trip, gave me a call to come up and take a look at what we were getting into. The swell was already about 8 or 10 feet and getting worse. I slowed the boat and let out more tow wire. It was too late to turn around and we spent the next 4 or 5 hours clawing our way towards Haro Strait to get into position to clear the shallow water off Smith Island and turn down wind for Rosario Strait.

It was dark, as usual, and we had two barges in tow. The conditions were bad enough that the radar was not able to pick up any distinct targets. We were trying to spot the south end of Lopez Island so we would know when to make our turn to go with the wind and swell into Rosario Straits. I thought I had spotted the right light and I thought we still had a ways to go. Then I realized it was the airport light on Lopez I was looking at. We were far enough and it was time to turn.

The wind was about 30 to 35 knots and we had 8 to 10 foot swells. Our turn would take some timing and coordination. I had Dave standby the tow wire brake and be prepared to let out wire so we could turn the boat without being restrained. I switched the steering to manual. We were going to try to make a quick turn between swells. With one spot light on the swell coming at us and one on the barges we waited for an opportunity. When I noticed two smaller waves coming I told Dave to start dropping wire and I put the rudder hard right and gave it some power. We came around fast and put the wind on our stern and avoided getting slammed by a wave. As soon as we had the swell on our stern we retightened the tow winch brake. Then I noticed on the radar that the two barges were merging, so I gave the tug more power and managed to pull the barges apart just before they collided.

The Strait of Georgia also threw rough weather at us from time to time. One evening as we were exiting the Fraser River with a heavily loaded 3,000-ton scrap metal barge, the southeast wind started to blow. At that point we had choices of three routes: Rosario Strait, Active Pass or Porlier Pass. I asked the crew who were all in the wheelhouse at the time, what their choice was. Rosario Strait would be slow going against the wind and the weather could get worse. Or head for Active Pass which would also be slow going and rough or Porlier Pass more protected and easier going but a longer route. They unanimously chose Porlier Pass which was downwind.

It took us about one and a half hours to get to the pass. The wind was blowing 30 knots. It was dark and raining and we had a 6 to 8 foot swell.

A 3000 ton barge

We shortened up the tow wire for the pass and made the turn to the port for the entrance. This put us sideways to the swell and because of the short wire we had to run slow. The heavy barge blew downwind which pulled the bow of the boat back into the wind. We were now moving side ways into the pass being pulled by the ebb current. With the length of the tug, barge and tow wire we were in danger of the barge hitting a reef on our starboard side. I had the mate watching the electronic chart with our track line on it and the deckhand running the spotlight. I was staying as close as I could to the rocks on the port side and holding my breath. As we got closer to the entrance to the pass we started to get out of the wind and the barge began to fall behind us, where it belonged.

I thought that would happen and I was right! But it gave us a thrill for a bit. After we got through the pass I said to Blaine, the mate, "That wasn't so bad," He said, "That was terrible. You are insane!" We both had a laugh! You might compare that experience to sitting at a stop light and when the light turns green you start to go and another car runs the red light and almost nails you. "Phew that was close!" Blaine was new with us. Even though he had a captain's license and 30 years experience in tug boating, we were still teaching him some new tricks.

Tugboat Life (2006 to 2010)
Chapter 58
Fraser River Challenges

The Fraser River presented several challenges for us with both empty and loaded barges. There were the tide and currents, wind, fog, shifting sand bars, all sizes of vessel traffic and, on two occasions, ice floes almost blocking the river.

The tide affects the river current for 40 or 50 miles upriver. In the spring (when ice and snow melt in the mountains), the flow increases from its normal 4 to 5 knots maximum to 6 to 8 knots in some of the areas we were transiting. In the spring we tried to time our arrivals at the mouth of the river on the flood tide. It could save us 3 to 4 hours in our 25 mile trip up the river when we traveled with the current.

At the mouth of the river, at Sand Heads, the current brings us almost to a stop at maximum ebb tide and there is a heavy cross current during the flood tide. The shove from the cross current pushes sideways. It is especially difficult at night when it is hard to detect and if you are not vigilant it pushes the barge into the navigation buoy on the south side of the entrance to the river.

The entrance to the Fraser River is unprotected from exposure to the wind. There is no protection for 4 or 5 miles up river. A rock jetty along the north side gives some protection from the swell. The south side is a shallow river delta that provides some protection from large waves. After exiting the river you are in the middle of the Strait of Georgia with long stretches of unprotected open water to the northwest and southeast.

I considered myself lucky when it came to fog. I never did have any bad fog experiences. The other crews did. Before I went to work on the *Anne Carlander* one crew had fog on a trip up the river. They were just able to sneak through the bridges before the bridge tender closed because of the fog. They had to wait a few hours for the fog to clear before heading back down river.

During the freshet season of snow melt, sand bars could develop because of the swift running current in the lower river. The pilots of the deep sea ships kept everyone informed of any developing problems.

The Fraser River is being dredged constantly year-round with two dredges to keep the navigation channels open. These dredges often created navigation problems all their own. They would not move for anyone. There were times when we were coming downriver with two loaded barges in tow and a dredge was working in a bend or a narrow area and other traffic from the other direction was arriving at that same spot. We tried to avoid arriving at the same time as other traffic but with two large heavy barges and going with the current it didn't always work out. We always managed to make it through okay but it was a nerve racking, white-knuckle event getting through those traffic tie-ups.

On most trips we saw deep sea ships transiting the river. We might get one or two trips and not see any, but the next trip we might have seen two or three on one transit up or down the river. The traffic system kept us advised by radio of all the traffic in the river. There were several places that we could move out of the navigation channel to accommodate ships passing if we had advance notice. In restricted areas the only option was to move as far to the right as possible to give them room to pass. It was a little tense to have those six to eight hundred foot ships (moving at ten knots) pass us as close as fifty feet.

The bridges at New Westminster could also get the adrenaline running. On one trip up the river with an empty barge I decided to use the south side of the bridge instead of the normal north side. As we started through, the current was running at a pretty lively clip, and the water was boiling through the slot. The boiling action started to throw the boat around and I "over-steered" while trying to keep up with it. Next thing I knew the tow wire, which we usually left out a few feet when transiting through the bridge, got off to the side and became hooked under the tug's rubber bumper on the stern. My forward motion had about stopped and we lay up against the center bridge wall. From there I was able to tow the barge on through the bridge and up to the Amix dock a few hundred yards with the wire still stuck under the bumper. We used a mobile crane from Amix to free the wire and the only damage was to the bumper. That was an easy fix.

We occasionally got the job of towing a 1x4 (400 feet long by 100 feet wide) barge empty from Tacoma to Amix. A larger tug was used to haul it loaded south bound, and we took it back empty. On the first trip northbound we expected to hand it off to assist tugs to take it through the bridges at New Westminster. This large barge was really pushing the limits of our capability. When we arrived at New Westminster the assist tugs refused to take the front end of the barge. After several phone calls we got the okay to take the front end ourselves. There was only about ten feet clearance on each side. That left no room for error. We managed to make it through without touching anything. We had two assist tugs, one on each side at the stern of the barge, and we put our two deckhands on the barge with radios to advise us of our clearance. It was a tight fit.

On two occasions the river was full of ice floes. It was never completely frozen over. There were just a lot of large floating islands of ice that was up to 6 inches thick and if we couldn't avoid them we had to crunch through them.

Even with the difficulties the Fraser River provided, I always enjoyed our trips up and down the river. I enjoyed its abundance of wildlife; ducks, geese, hawks, eagles, seals, sea lions, fish, and its ever-changing moods - sometimes calm and peaceful other times wild and restless.

Tugboat Life (2006 to 2010)
Chapter 59
Three Incidents that got the Attention of the Coast Guard

In the summer of 2010 we had three non-weather incidents that got the attention of the US Coast Guard. The first one occurred on a nice Sunday evening, warm with a light, northwest wind blowing. We left Tacoma with one empty barge in tow for Surrey, B.C., and because it was one of our large barges we had about 800 feet of wire out.

I was on watch when we were passing Shilshole Marina (just north of Seattle) at about 1700. I noticed a large sailing vessel approaching from the area of Port Madison towards Shilshole Marina, about one mile ahead on my port side at about a 45 degree angle. I picked up the binoculars and took a look at her. She was about 60 feet with two masts and had her sails up. I could see one man steering at the aft helm station and I knew he could see me.

It's common to encounter a large numbers of small vessels and sailboats in that area. Over the years dealing with sailboats, if they are on a course with favorable wind they tend not to want to turn until the last minute. As she passed abeam of us at about 200 yards she still had not changed course. Now I was getting concerned and looked him over again. The man was still sitting at the wheel and my thought was, "He is going to cross my tow wire."

I pulled the throttle back to idle to let the tow wire drop down, I was mesmerized as I watched him plow head first into the side of my barge about 30 feet back from the bow. She hit at a 45 degree angle; his whole boat shook and ricocheted to the right, and slid side by side down the full length of the barge. "OH SHIT!" I think the reason he didn't turn was because his sails were blocking his view of the barge. Why he didn't see the tow wire leading off our stern is hard to say!

All the crew members who were down in the galley came running up to see what was going on. I immediately checked my position on the electronic chart and called the Coast Guard to let them know what had happened. We shortened our tow wire and headed back to see if the sailboat need assistance. The Coast Guard wanted us to call them on the phone and asked us if we could tell the captain on the sailboat to do the same.

We approached the sailboat close enough to holler across and ask him if he was okay and passed on the information from the Coast Guard. He said he was okay! The "bowsprit" (a long pole that sticks out forward from the bow to hold the forward jib sail) was broken and crumpled up but that was the only damage we could see from the starboard side. There was nothing more we could do so we got underway again. I had an Incident Report to fill out and forward to the Coast Guard.

About four weeks later I received a letter from the Coast Guard informing me that they would be placing a letter into my file that charged me with failure to take all necessary action to avoid the collision. My failure was I had not blown a danger signal on the tug's horn before the collision. I called them to protest their action but got nowhere. I asked what about the other guy who made all the wrong moves. I was told that he would be getting a lot worse than I had.

The Rules Of The Road state in Rule 10 that a small vessel or sailing vessel shall not impede the safe passage of a power driven vessel following the traffic lanes - and we had been in the lanes.

The next incident occurred about a month later. We were southbound for Tacoma with one of our largest barges loaded with scrap metal. At about 0500 as we approached the traffic buoy off the north end of the Seattle harbor, Steve was on watch and I was in bed sleeping. All of a sudden I was awakened by a loud scraping sound and the tug lurched to a stop. Even though I came out of a deep sleep I knew we had run aground and I also knew that the barge would be heading at us.

I charged out of bed not even bothering to get dressed. I ran up the stairs into the dark wheelhouse and out the back door onto the upper deck to the control station. I shined the spotlight on the barge and it was headed straight for us.

I hadn't seen Steve in the dark. He was in the wheelhouse trying to back the tug off the beach. This had all taken two or three minutes since we hit the beach. I yelled, "Steve give us some wheel wash." We needed to push a strong wheel wash out from the stern to intercept the barge and cause it to change course. He yelled back, "I am!" I said, "No, not in reverse, Put it in forward. The barge is going to run into us." He suddenly realized what I was saying, shifted to forward, and added power. Just in time the barge ran into the wheel wash and turned enough to miss us and slid to a stop about 25 feet to our left.

The last thing Steve remembered was approaching the change of course at the traffic buoy at the north side of the Seattle harbor. The deckhand was down in the galley and he was alone in the wheelhouse when he fell sound asleep. He woke up when we hit the beach at Yeomalt Point.

'Tug On Beach' (*Kitsap Sun* – Eric Fredrick) Sep 10, 2010

After I got dressed I went back to the wheelhouse where Steve was still trying to back off the beach. I suggested he move the rudder back and forth, which would rock the boat side to side to help get us get moving. He tried but the rudder would not move.

I went down to the back deck and found our longest pike pole to measure the water depth at our stern and found it to be more than 13 feet which was our maximum depth. That was strange, what was wrong with the rudder? It had enough water. Meanwhile in the wheelhouse, Steve was still trying to back off the beach while talking to the Coast Guard.

It was still dark and I was hoping we could get out of there before daylight. Then I noticed several people had already gathered on the beach and at least one man was taking pictures.

When I got back up to the wheelhouse, Steve suddenly remembered that he had forgotten to turn off the auto pilot and that was the reason the rudder would not move. As soon as he turned the manual steering on the rudder responded. By moving it from side to side we slid off the beach. We hooked on to the stern of the barge with a soft line and easily pulled it off the beach as well.

This was probably the best place in Puget Sound to run aground. The beach was steep and all gravel, so even though the bow was aground the stern was not touching bottom. The only damage was some paint scraped off the bottom hull.

After a short wait for the Coast Guard to release us we continued underway. We arrived in Tacoma where we were met by Coast Guard investigators. One came aboard with a big smile on his face. He said he lived a few houses down from where we ran aground and had been out on the beach watching us. Good thing we reported it.

The third incident occurred in Tacoma harbor. Our main engine on the *Anne Carlander* died as we were about to pull tow wire in. The weather was calm, and we were in no danger of running aground or colliding with anything. We called Foss for an assist and drifted around for about 30 minutes until they got to us. While we were waiting we pulled in the tow wire and tied the tug alongside the barge. They hauled us and our barge to our dock and tied us up. After some repairs to the fuel system we were back in action after only a few days.

Because these incidents all occurred within a short period of time the Coast Guard required the company owner to jump through some hoops to continue to operate.

Tugboat Life (2006 to 2010)
Chapter 60
The Last Trip and Retirement

As we got into 2010 and I turned 70 I started thinking seriously about retiring. I didn't want to stay at it too long, end up retiring after my health had deteriorated and miss out on some of my golden years. I had been working since 1959 but was still not tired of what I was doing. I still enjoyed the challenge. By this time I had worked at four different companies, Dunlap Towing, Puget Sound Freight Lines, Olympic Tug and Barge and Pacific Northwest Marine Services.

Dunlap had given me my first job and I am forever grateful to them for that opportunity. It was a tough decision when I decided to go with Puget Sound Freight Lines when the two companies split.

At Puget Sound Freight Lines we had started a new division in an older company and it was exciting to be part of a new, growing enterprise. When Puget Sound ran its course after 28 years and decided to go out of business I was forced into a transition to Olympic Tug and Barge.

Olympic was different than what I had been used to. As part of the oil transportation business we had a lot of regulations to deal with. Management was more in your face and some managers were hard to deal with. After a few years I started to look around for new opportunities. One presented itself when a captain at Pacific Northwest Marine Services resigned.

Pacific Northwest Marine Services turned out to be the right job at the right time for me. It was a combination of simplicity and challenges at the same time. The simplicity part amounted to one crew and one manager who all worked well together. The challenging part was dealing with multiple barges in one tow and the sometimes rough open, wide waters of the Strait of Juan de Fuca and Strait of Georgia, plus the confined area and tricky currents of the Fraser River.

As the summer months of 2010 rolled by, I started mentioning to the crew members that I might retire at the end of the year. I finally brought the subject up with the owner and his first reaction was, "No you don't want to do that! What would you do with yourself?" After some discussion on the subject I agreed to be available for relief captain service after I retired and set the first part of December as the date.

I finally announced to everyone that the trip on the 11th of December would be my final one. It turned out to be a routine one barge up and one barge back. When we returned to Tacoma on the 12th I removed my personal possessions from the tug and headed home. There was the thrill of, "Wow! I've finely done it!" But at the same time I wondered how this new "retirement" thing was going to turn out?

I was relieving Steve about once a month when he needed time off until March of 2011. Then one morning I got a call from Steve and he said that they had just crewed up for a trip and Dave was there for a crew meeting. Dave informed them that he had just sold the company and this would be their final trip. They would leave the tug at New Westminster. Dave would be there to take them back home. Wow what a bolt out of the blue! He explained that he had been forced into the sale by the owner of the scrap metal company in Canada which had happened just the week before.

The next morning I got a call from Luke, one of the deckhands. They had tied up the *Anne Carlander* and were just leaving New Westminster for Tacoma. I agreed to meet them for lunch at the Conway Pub when they got down to Mount Vernon. When they arrived at the Pub they presented me with the ship's brass bell as a retirement gift. After lunch and some reminiscing about the good times we had had they went on their way.

Two of the crewmembers went to work immediately at other tug companies. Steve, the captain, took some time off before going back to tug boating. One deckhand worked several jobs for a year then went back to work on tugboats. Once you have put your feet on one of these hard working boats and traveled around on the water it's hard to get away from!

Over the 50 years of my working career I've seen the towboat industry change from the use of small wooden, single screw tugs to the powerful twin screw steel hull tugs of today. Navigation has changed from a magnetic compass, a spotlight and paper charts to today's electronic gadgets. VHF radios, cell phones, radar, electronic charts, GPS (Global Positioning Satellites), AIS (Automatic Identification System) and close scrutiny by the Coast Guard and management. In the days when I started towboating there was very little contact with the outside world until you got to a dock with a pay phone or arrived back at your home port.

Spending half of my life at work on the water I missed lots of occasions, parties, weddings, funerals, childbirths, graduations and the normal nine to five working routine. Today's tug boaters all have cell phones and are in contact with family and friends as long as they are in sight of land. Whether this is an improvement depends on who you talk to. There were times over the years that I wondered if I had chosen the right career, but looking back on it now I wouldn't trade it for anything.

THE END

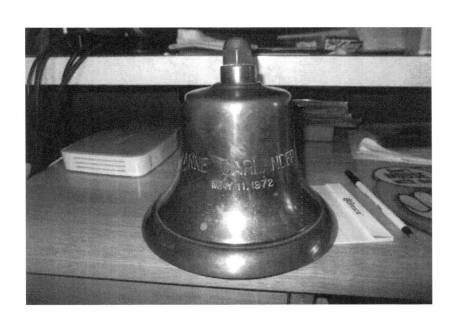

Brass Bell
From *Anne Carlander*
Retirement gift from David Joseph and crew of *Anne Carlander*.

List of tugs I was Captain on in 4 companies

1- Vulcan
2- Malolo
3- Pacific Foam
4- Crosmor
5- Narada
6- Kiket
7- Edith Lovejoy
8- Anne Carlander
9- Pachena
10- Duwamish
11- Catherine Quigg
12- Alyssa Ann
13- Lela Joy

Tugs I spent a brief time on

14- Martha Foss
15- Pacific Falcon
16- Millennium Star
17- CF Campbell
18- Max Sodland

A career spanning from single screw wooden tugs, to single screw steel hulled, to twin screw tugs and then tractor tugs

Captain Gerald Bell